Living Among Wolves

A Historical Fiction/Biography

by
Kurt Hahn

Copyright © 2013 by Kurt Hahn

All rights reserved.

ISBN-10: 1482655624
EAN-13: 9781482655629
Library of Congress Control Number: 2013904327
CreateSpace Independent Publishing Platform,
North Charleston, SC

Dedication

This book is dedicated to all survivors of human atrocities and inhumane savagery. To those who were forced to leave their countries, homes, and families. To the memory of those victims who died at the hands of fellow humans who were driven by devilish ideologies or greed. To the heroes pushed to the edge of their physical, emotional, and mental strength to save their fellow man. To those who sacrificed their dignity just to stay alive. To those betrayed and disillusioned, who struggle to regain faith in humanity as they endeavor to rebuild their lives. To those who cannot verbalize their horrors. May this book speak the unspeakable.

Table of Contents

Prologue..vii
Author's Note...ix
Chapter 1: Genesis..1
Chapter 2: The Danger of Security...15
Chapter 3: The Frankfurter Judengasse.................................25
Chapter 4: The Journey to the Sea...39
Chapter 5: The Manna..45
Chapter 6: Crossing the Sea...51
Chapter 7: Entry into the Promised Land..............................67
Chapter 8: St. Petersburg, 1756...73
Chapter 9: Go and Take Possession of the Good Land.......107
Chapter 10: A Troubled Paradise...113
Chapter 11: Chameleonic Paradise.......................................137
Chapter 12: In the Shadows of Pogroms..............................153
Chapter 13: From the Fry Pan into the Fire.........................173
Chapter 14: Peace and War...183
Chapter 15: Rail Tracks of Life and Death..........................197
Epilogue..205

Prologue

WOLVES—these cunning, cautious but persistent predators hunt in packs. They can scent prey over very long distances pursue it until they have made their kill. Their howl, which may have more power to stir human emotions than any other animal cry, can strike terror in the heart of their prey. Yet none are as fearful or savage as the "wolves" of the human variety. The similarities of such people to wolves can hardly escape the notice of the reader. When these act as a pack, the "pack mentality" takes hold of them.

In his book *Extraordinary Popular Delusions and the Madness of Crowds* (1841), Scottish journalist Charles MacKay states, "Men, it has been well said, think in herds. It will be seen that they go mad in herds, while they only recover their senses slowly and one by one." There is no logic or compassion when they attack. They are not easily dissuaded from their course of action. "Howling" like wolves, they scream and shout to drown any dissenting voices and send innocent people panicking into traps, while at the same time they feed the raging emotions that will whip them into frenzy. On the other hand, the lone wolf, usually an old, ostracized female of the pack, is a desperate predator who, out of necessity, will take greater risk to get her prey. She may become so intent on her victim that she does not see the dangers lurking for her.

Living among such people requires equal cunning. For an intended or targeted victim, the constant mental mode is survival. This deep-seated instinct drives everything, sometimes with cold, calculated reason, and at other times, in the heat of the moment, with sheer desperation. You know the "wolves" are there. By necessity, you may have to share their environment. But you do not know exactly where they are or when they will strike. This X factor of uncertainty in itself makes each victim vulnerable. When you come face-to-face with the wolves, there are only two possible outcomes: triumph or tragedy; live or die. To live, you have to stand up to them and not let them dictate the terms of how you live among them. That is the great challenge.

Author's Note

FOR MANY YEARS OF MY early life, I didn't know that I had what others called grandfathers. I knew only mothers, grandmothers, and great-grandmother, but the concept of a father, let alone a grandfather, was totally foreign to me. Except for my brothers and the boys in my neighbourhood I knew only women, because all men were at war, including my father and his brothers. Max and Paul died on the battlefields. Horst was badly wounded and spent more time after the war in hospitals than at home. Richard was a prisoner of war in Russia for nine years after the war. Two of my mother's brothers also did not return from the war. Hence, on one occasion, I was told that when my father arrived home on leave from the army, I called him Aunty, which did not impress him. Only when I began my schooling I learned that everyone has two grandfathers, even great-grandfathers. Then I met some of those mysterious creatures called grandfathers. My friend living two houses away had one of those.

All this awoke in me a powerful curiosity. Who were these men whose genes I was made of? What had I inherited from them? What did they look like, and how did they speak? What work did they do, and were they good at it? What other children did these ancestors of mine have, and where did they live? My mind flooded with a torrent of questions like these. As I grew older, they teased and tormented me.

Sometimes I would imagine what these relatives looked like. There was one photo of my maternal grandfather, Gustav Janutta, who was killed on the battlefield on August 17, 1917, in Kowel, Russia, but none of my paternal grandfather, Friedrich Hahn, who was born in Russia and died in East Prussia. The only way to get answers those days—that is, in the late 1940s and '50s—was from my parents and grandmothers.

My father, who himself lived a tormented life, as we shall see later, was a closed book on family history, barring a few snippets of his early life. His father died a broken man when my father was just twenty years old. On my mother's side, there was a little more information. However, I am not surprised that she did not tell me much about her father, either. When he was killed in battle in 1917, my mother was barely eleven years old. She hardly knew him herself. What information was given to me was more cryptic than descriptive. There were bits thrown to me, as one who feeds a begging puppy—pieces of information, often deliberately edited versions, without connections to other events. I suppose it is a bit like giving sex education to a child: you tell it what you think it needs at the time, without all the graphic details. Perhaps my elders feared loading an inquisitive mind with too much, even explosive, information that might be considered damaging to a child. Nevertheless, it was Grandma Pauline, my father's mother, the oral historian in the family, who gradually supplied most of these bits of information to me. As the baby in the family, I always slept in the same room as my two grandmothers. Often Grandma Pauline would reminisce and ramble on about random stories of her childhood, names, places, and events that made little sense to my childish mind. Some stories seemed wildly exaggerated, tending toward the mysterious, while others were merely facts. As a child, I was reasonably able to separate fact from fiction. However, many stories stuck in my mind, and, like a dog that cannot let go of its bone, my fertile imagination happily filled in all the gaps when I was alone, such as the details of my ancestors' lives, the houses

Author's Note

they lived in, and the clothes they wore. Years later, my research confirmed the veracity of many of Grandma Pauline's stories. But there was one major event that finally helped to put some pieces of my "jigsaw puzzle life" together.

When Mother died, she told us that my father was Jewish; more specifically, his father was a Jew. This was a secret kept well under wraps for "safety's sake." However, it suddenly linked a lot of those "jigsaw puzzle pieces" of information and caused in me an avalanche of desire to learn more about my father's family. I wanted to see the whole picture. I wanted these dead men and women of the past to come alive. I wanted to hear them speak and express their hopes, loves, and fears. The historical events they had lived through were real, and the human emotions that they must have experienced were real. I wanted to hear them tell me their stories, and wanted to share in their tears and laughter. In doing research, I established a number of historical dates and names. My imagination filled in the rest, thus re-creating or reinventing the characters that were my ancestors. This book is a historical fiction based on actual historical events interwoven with confirmed facts and family anecdotes. *Living Among Wolves* puts a human face to some well-known and lesser known historical events that are recorded as cold and faceless facts of history.

So begins the story of *Living Among Wolves*. It is a story of anti-Semitism, persecution, desperation, betrayal, disappointment, unbelievable heartbreak, hatred, genocide, death and survival. It is also a story of human heroics, love, forgiveness, tender compassion, hope, and life. It is a story of meeting challenges on a harsh frontier with all sorts of adversity. Although the theme of anti-Semitism is as old as the Bible, for me it is in the city of Ludwigsburg, in Baden-Württemberg, Germany, where the story begins.

Kurt Hahn

Chapter 1
Genesis

"They hate whom they fear." —Thyestes

THE FOUNDATION STONE OF LUDWIGSBURG Palace, a showpiece of opulence and splendor in eighteenth-century Württemberg, was laid on May 17, 1704, by Eberhard Ludwig, the Duke of Württemberg. Five years later, the Duke established the city of Ludwigsburg only twelve kilometres north of Stuttgart, hitherto the residence of the Duke. The earliest residents of the city were the workers and artisans who built the palace. The Duke founded the city of Ludwigsburg to stamp his authority as the absolute monarch. The distance from his palace to the new city of Ludwigsburg was exactly the same distance as the Palace of Versailles is from Paris. Thus, Ludwigsburg Palace, with its magnificent gardens, has been referred to as the "Versailles of southern Germany."

Because of its noble status, the city of Ludwigsburg held great attraction to philosophers and the intelligentsia of Württemberg. For the same reason, it attracted shrewd businessmen and bankers, some of them Jews. Hence, Ludwigsburg became a prosperous city that provided employment for outstanding craftsmen and artisans who settled there to ply their skills. Ludwigsburg must have experienced phenomenal growth, for in just nine years, by 1718, the city became the capital and sole residence of the dukes of Württemberg for a period of time. In an environment of such abundant wealth, the line between astute business practice and greed can become increasingly blurred, often leading to jealousy, revenge, and bloodshed, and creating an abrasive environment of mistrust that exposes the fragile threads of loyalty like the bare linen strands of a well-worn rag.

On this particular cold February day, most of the businesses have closed before nightfall, as is customary. Only a few of the trade workshops remain open for a little while longer; then the craftsmen, too, make their way home. Ludwigsburg is shutting down for the night. The streetlights on the cobblestone side street, aptly named Steinbeistraße, were lit at dusk by the lamplighter. These lights now cast forlorn shadows of people trudging home in the cold winter air, as they wrap their scarves and the collars of their coats more tightly around their necks. In the distance is the sound of an old nag dragging her tired feet over the cobblestone street, pulling a wagon, weary from the day's toil. Somewhere a dog barks in its boredom. The bland and stupefying moon adds to the mood of a jaded city wanting to get its rest.

The city's renowned coachbuilder, Itzhak, has worked much later than usual today. He, too, is tired. Nevertheless, he meticulously puts all his cleaned tools in their proper place, a good habit he learned from his father. As he carefully extinguishes the lights, he muses for a few moments in the workshop where he worked with his father, Salomon, who came here from Stuttgart to Ludwigsburg at the invitation of the Duke, building magnificent coaches for the Duke and his court. Memories of that happy time warm Itzhak's heart. He thinks about the other apprentice his father had, Vladimir, with whom he practically grew up. He wonders whatever happened to Vladimir and where he is now. Peace, prosperity, and goodwill were the hallmark of those earlier years in Ludwigsburg.

"Ah, yes, peace," he mumbles with a deep sigh as his thoughts turn to an incident a few days earlier, when a group of youths gathered like a pack of wolves and threw rocks into his workshop. It was a very measured attack. They could have caused far more damage than they did. It seemed to him as if it was orchestrated just to intimidate.

Once outside, he shuts the workshop and looks at the damaged door. He will repair it tomorrow. Suddenly, a horse-drawn coach pulls up behind him and interrupts his thoughts. Looking around, he smiles to himself with a measure of pride as he recognizes the coach as one from his workshop. It is easily identifiable because of its brass insignia of a rooster, the German word for which is *Hahn*.

"Good evening, Itzhak," says a familiar voice from inside the coach, as it comes to a stop.

Itzhak strains his eyes in the semidarkness to see who is in the coach.

"How is my favorite brother-in-law?" the voice says. "Is all well?"

"Oh…, hello Baruch. Yes, yes, of course, all is well…enough… at the moment," he replies haltingly.

"No, no, Itzhak, no"—Baruch waves his index finger as a way of chastisement—"all is not well, and you know that. The whole of Baden-Württemberg is becoming a dangerous place for us Jews. Of course, we are no strangers to religious intolerance, but this one could turn ugly." He points to the damaged door of the workshop. "Come, I'll give you a ride home."

The springs of the coach squeak as Itzhak launches his large frame onto the leather seat next to the well-rounded figure of his brother-in-law. The perfectly constructed door shuts with a gentle *click* that gives him a feeling of deep satisfaction. "What brings you out to this side of town tonight, Baruch?"

"I had a meeting—business, you know—with the chief magistrate. He needed a little 'help,' if you know what I mean. And for us Jews, it pays to have friends in the right places, but never mind that."

Itzhak looks at his well-to-do relative Baruch Goldstein, the financier, who is staring straight ahead.

"Ever since the great diaspora," Goldstein begins like a grand orator, "we Jews have always been on the run. Sometimes we were forced to leave, like when Spain and France expelled the Jews, while other times we thought it safer to leave on our own terms—"

"Is this one of your history lessons, Baruch?" Itzhak interrupts.

"No, I'm sorry if I bore you," Baruch says, in a could-not-care-less tone, while looking the other way out of the coach.

"And your point is...?"

"Do you know what date is it today, Itzhak Hahn?"

"February fourth 1743. I am hungry and tired, and tomorrow is the fifth, and I have to get up early and work again," Itzhak replied in a grumpy sort of a way.

"Yes, Itzhak, you are always so practical, with your head down to work, and to hell with the rest of the world. I mean no offense, Itzhak, but what is really significant about this date?"

"*What?*" says Itzhak, still a little annoyed.

"It is exactly four years since they executed the Jew Joseph SüßOppenheimer in Stuttgart. 'Jud Süß,' the crowd shouted, taunting him at his public hanging." Baruch's voice resounds with suppressed anger. As a banker, he had much to do with Oppenheimer and his reform measures, which made Oppenheimer a lot of enemies but made Baruch a lot of money. "And his corpse is still hanging exhibited in a wire cage just outside of Stuttgart these four years on, and who knows how many more years—what is that saying to you...to us all?"

Both men remain silent for a few moments as the coach continues rattling rhythmically across the cobblestones, the sound of which seems like a thousand hammers relentlessly bashing that image of Joseph Süß into the men's consciousness. "I did not come past your workshop by accident," Baruch says, breaking the silence.

"I thought as much," replies Itzhak casually.

"I want to talk to you, Itzhak—I need to talk to you seriously. I worry about you, my sister, Esther, and my little nephew. I worry about all of us here."

Itzhak looks questioningly at Baruch, and their eyes meet. "What is troubling you, Baruch?"

Again, looking out of the coach window as if ensuring that no listening ears are nearby, Baruch begins without looking back at Itzhak. "Come, Itzhak, as if you don't know what's troubling us Jews right now. But never mind that." He pauses for a moment. His well-rounded body shifts uneasily around on the leather seat, but then he composes himself and goes on in his oratory style. "I recently went to Buchau, where I had dinner with the highly respected Einstein family, who live in the Hofgarten Straße 14—the Judengasse [Jewish ghetto]—and with a number of other notable Jews who live there. In that circle of intellectuals and financiers, we discussed the astounding, and, may I say, rapid, improvements in Russian politics and economy implemented by Tsar Peter the Great since the early 1720s. He transformed Russia and set it on a path to becoming a potent force in Europe. He was a great visionary."

"Come to the point, Baruch," Itzhak says impatiently.

"Fine, fine," Baruch says picking up on Itzhak's irritation. "Do you feel safe here? What about Esther and your son, Joachim? Do you see a good life for them in this land of 'wolves'?" He pauses. "Bingo!" He knows he has struck deeply into Itzhak's consciousness. God knows how many times he has silently asked himself these questions that have tormented his soul. Itzhak is well aware of the fluctuating fortunes of the Jews in Baden-Württemberg. One moment they are free to trade, free to settle in the cities, favored by the nobility; the next they are banned and ordered to live in the Judengassen. Generally they are hated, and some even executed like common criminals, by those who fear Jewish success.

"There *is* a safe place to go to—Russia—and many Jews from Buchau, Stuttgart, Heidelberg, and other places are already making plans to emigrate," Baruch continues. "There is security for families and big money to be made in Russia—think about it, Itzhak!" He knows not to say anything further; Itzhak is a proud, stubborn, and very impatient man.

The coach halts near Itzhak's home. When he opens the door, a rush of the cold air catches his breath and he coughs a few times.

"You should see about this cough of yours; you've had it for a while now." Baruch's voice takes on a fatherly tone.

"No, no, it is nothing, Baruch. Thank you for the lift. Give my regards to your wife, Golda." Still coughing, he jumps out and his hulky body quickly disappears in the dark night. The rhythmic *clip-clop* of trotting horseshoes clanging against the cobblestones, vanishing in the distance, seems to say to Itzhak, *Russia-Russia-Russia*. Esther will be waiting for him inside.

Esther was born on July 22, 1717, in Stuttgart. She and her brother, Baruch, were raised in the Goldstein family, relatives of the Mendelssohn's musical and banking family. Both were highly educated. Besides her very articulate German and Yiddish, Esther spoke French fluently and had a good grasp of Russian. Music was a prominent part of the Goldstein's' social life. Esther displayed a particular talent for the violin and studied music under some of Stuttgart's finest violinists. Her father bought a violin for her from a friend who had little interest in music, for a reasonable price. At a young age, she became a member of the Stuttgart Orchestra and was featured in a number of solo performances. She was a rising star on the Stuttgart music scene. She also inherited the Mendelssohn's business acumen.

Itzhak met Esther in the synagogue in Stuttgart on his frequent trips there to buy wood for his father's workshop. They were married in Stuttgart in 1740, two years after his father, Salomon, died. Esther immediately took charge of the business's financial arrangements, and that proved to be a blessing, as Itzhak's business began to make good profits. Nevertheless, her heart was in music performance, and she worked with an ensemble in Ludwigsburg and with her old connections in Stuttgart. However, when their son,

Joachim Henrik, was born on March 7, 1742, Esther's involvement in the music scene became quite limited.

A rush of warm air greets him inside the house. The fireplace is aglow, and the sudden change of temperature brings on another coughing attack. Elegant Esther looks concerned. "How was your day at the workshop?"

"As usual—nothing out of the ordinary."

"I mean, was there any more trouble?" she asks with an expectant look on her face.

"No need to worry, Esther. All is settling down well. It was just a prank by some stupid, idle youths." Itzhak's voice has a mellow, most reassuring tone that immediately relieves her anxiety. "Our Joachim will soon be one year old," Itzhak says with a measure of pride and prompted by recalling his conversation with Baruch.

"I know, Itzhak, I'm a mother. Mothers never forget their children's day of birth." Yet there will be nothing in the house that indicates any kind of celebration. Not because they are poor, but because, according to the oldest Jewish traditions, as noted by the historian Josephus, Jews do not celebrate birthdays. While some Jews do celebrate them in their own way, Itzhak and Esther remain resolved to uphold the old tradition. Itzhak walks into the room where his son is sleeping. Esther's violin lies nearby. She always plays soft lullabies for Joachim, which he loves. Then he goes off into a blissful sleep. Itzhak's huge hand gently holds his son's little fingers. As he looks adoringly at his son, again the words of Baruch Goldstein race through his mind. *Perhaps he is right,* he thinks; *perhaps there is more trouble brewing. Baruch seemed so certain of it.* He reflects on an uneasiness he has never seen before in Baruch. He coughs again, and the baby stirs. He quickly leaves the room so as not to disturb the sleeping child.

Back in the kitchen, Esther has made him a drink of hot chicken broth. "Drink—it will be good for your cough," she says as she pushes the mug to him.

He takes a satisfying sip and leans back in his chair. "I saw your brother, Baruch, today. He gave me a ride home in the new coach I built for him. I think his money-lending business makes him a good income." The hot broth is warming his chest, easing the urge to cough.

Esther is at the kitchen bench, preparing *Abendbrot*, the typical German evening meal, except, of course, that all their food is kosher. "What did you talk about in the coach?" she asks without turning around.

This direct question startles Itzhak. "Why do you ask such a question? We just chatted about…this and that."

"Itzhak! I know my brother—he just doesn't chat about 'this and that.' Lately he seems to have something heavy on his mind. Golda told me that Baruch is concerned about the religious and racial unrest in the district. We all expected trouble today on this fourth anniversary of the murder of Oppenheimer."

"Yes, unusually quiet," Itzhak half mumbles to himself.

After the evening meal, Esther checks on Joachim, and then they both go to bed, where Itzhak reveals to Esther his conversation with Baruch. Assuring Esther that all is well, he gently kisses her forehead and says, "Good night." After much quiet soul searching, Itzhak also drops off to sleep.

Something wakes him just after midnight. He listens carefully but cannot make out what it is. He gets out of bed and looks through the window and sees an orange glow in the distance. It seems as if a building is on fire. His heart suddenly races as he calculates that the fire is in the direction of his workshop. He is trying to convince himself that it is not, and gets back to bed, but he cannot sleep.

Suddenly, a sharp rapping on the front door makes him jump out of bed and run toward the front door. He sees Baruch standing there, breathless and frantically waving him to jump into the coach. He obviously does not want to disturb the neighbors. Panicking now, Itzhak grabs his heavy coat and throws it over his shoulders, picks up his boots, and jumps into the coach, where he has another coughing fit. The two men look at each other, speechless. They both know what is happening. The coach suddenly jerks forward and flings the men's heads back as the coachman drives the horse hard.

In a few minutes, they arrive at the top of the street, from where they can see the workshop ablaze. They dare not go any closer.

"Maybe it was an accident," Itzhak stammers from fear and the freezing cold.

"An accident?" Baruch bellows. "Are you mad, Itzhak? Don't you see the young men dancing and shouting, 'Jud Süß'? Anyone of us can be the next 'Jud Süß.' Tonight you're the one, Itzhak."

Itzhak's head falls into his large hands, and he lets out a few German expletives. In his anger, he attempts to jump out of the coach and run down the street to deal with the men. Baruch holds him back, and Itzhak begins to sob uncontrollably. The memories of his father establishing the workshop and how much time Itzhak spent with him learning the trade—all of it gone, up in smoke. His whole world collapses at that moment into an unbearable heap of despair.

Baruch turns the coach around to head back home. "Itzhak, you and your family are leaving tonight. Pack what you can and load it into the coach, but do it quietly. We do not want to wake the neighbors."

"But where can I go—Russia?" Itzhak asks sarcastically.

"Yes, but not tonight. I will take you and your family to Frankfurt. We should get there in a day or so. I have a good friend there who will take care of you for a couple of weeks. I will sort out your affairs in Ludwigsburg—I have connections, as you know—and I will come to you after I collect whatever money is owed to you, as well as your savings and your belongings that can be salvaged.

Then we can sit down and make some rational plans, but, yes, Russia will probably be it, and Golda and I are coming with you. We shall start a new life again, together. So go inside and wake up Esther and explain to her the urgency of this situation. Then quietly pack the essentials that you will need for the next two weeks. Bring all your business documents. They will be safer with me than being left in the house. I will be here at three a.m. so you have two hours to pack."

"By the way, Baruch, how did you get to know about the fire so quickly, in the middle of the night?"

"Let's just say I did," Baruch answers tersely.

Itzhak opens the door, and there stands Esther, trembling, eyes brimming with tears "It was the workshop, Itzhak, wasn't it? When you left the house, I got out of bed and saw the fire. I am terrified, Itzhak—what is happening?"

Itzhak takes his dear Esther into his arms, and they both dissolve in tears. He then tells her of Baruch's plan. They hastily put some of their belongings together. Esther lovingly packs her violin and some of her music library. When Baruch arrives, they quietly leave the house with Joachim.

The Erlingers live next door. They are recently married. Johanna is only seventeen years old, while her husband, Dietmar, is almost forty. Since the beginning, it has been a turbulent marriage, with much quarrelling and abuse. Because Johanna is young and attractive, Dietmar becomes very jealous if another male so much as looks at her, and he is always suspicious of his wife's fidelity, especially when he is drunk, and that is very often. Johanna frequently confides in Esther, who acts like an older sister to her.

The curtain in the Erlinger's home next door moves briefly. Esther thinks she sees Johanna Erlinger at the window but cannot be certain. Other than that, no one else seems to notice their departure.

The coach begins to move ever so slowly to reduce the noise, until they are a few houses away. Esther looks tearfully back at what was their happy home. Everything is asleep except for that lone figure in the window of the Erlinger's house. Then the coach slips away around the next corner. Baruch looks out the back window. No one seems to follow them. Soon they cross the bridge over the river Neckar, and then they are heading northward. Their visibility is good until a light snow begins to fall, reducing the moonlight to an eerie haze. The air is deathly still, barring the rattling of the coach and horse.

About an hour later, Baruch stops the coach. "Quiet! Listen!" He motions with his finger across his lips. The barely perceptible sound of galloping horses vibrates through the still night air. Baruch quickly instructs the coachman to take them into the forest on the side of the road.

Baruch jumps out of the coach. He grabs a fallen branch from a fir tree and sweeps over the tracks the coach and his footprints left, which are quite visible in the new snow. Hidden in the forest, the group waits. A few minutes later, two horses gallop by. Itzhak then wants to move on, but Baruch counsels him to wait until the riders return. That proves to be good advice, for a little while later they come back, confirming Baruch's suspicion that these men are looking for them. With horror, the travellers hold their breath as the horses slow down and then stop threateningly close to their cover.

"Erlinger, are you sure that they left on this road?" a rough voice inquires. Esther can hardly believe her ears; Johanna Erlinger was her good neighbor. They helped each other when necessary. Esther feels stabbed in the heart. "So they watched us as we left," she says quietly.

Erlinger looks around. The now-heavy snow has covered any possible tracks that may have been visible before. "Maybe I was wrong," Erlinger says disappointedly. "We'd better get home before the snowfall becomes too heavy. We are patient, and we will get that Jew yet." The sounds of the horses vanish in the distance.

Baruch waits until there is no chance that the riders will hear their coach. Relieved that they remained undetected, they proceed toward Frankfurt. "Itzhak, do you believe me now that our lives were in danger in Ludwigsburg?" Baruch asks.

Itzhak just nods his head in agreement. Yet he is puzzled about why they want to kill him. Aside from being a Jew, he minded his own business and built coaches. A dreadful reality now sets in: life as the Hahns and the Goldsteins knew it will never be the same again.

"Where did your husband go? And why did he take Itzhak and Esther?" roars the man with the rough voice. With their faces covered, the two men tower over diminutive Golda Goldstein, who has no idea what is going on. All she knows is that Baruch has gone into Ludwigsburg on some urgent business before picking up the Hahns. "Who did he see in Ludwigsburg? Speak, woman!" The knife presses harder on her throat as the questioning intensifies. "Did you see what your husband loaded into the coach?"

"No!" Then Golda lets out a scream as the sharp tip of the knife punctures her skin slightly.

A large hand covering her mouth instantly stifles her scream. The man draws the knife back and shows Golda a drop of blood on the tip. "If you dare to scream again, that will be the last thing you will do on God's Earth," he threatens her. When he steps back, she grabs her neck and feels the warm blood on her fingers. She shudders. "You'd better start thinking. We will be back in a few hours. And don't think about running away. We are watching you." With that, he jerks her by the arm and drags her to the window. In the first light of dawn, she sees a group of young men waiting menacingly outside her house.

As it becomes daylight, Golda sees a coach pull up in front of her house. Four men get out, and the youths quickly disperse as they recognize the chief magistrate and three police officers. *What are they doing here?* Golda asks herself. *Will they arrest me and take me away?* Her fear wells up in her heart, which begins to pound faster and faster as the men enter the house. At the sight of the men Golda collapses and faints.

When she recovers, she recognizes Karl Sieger, the chief magistrate and a good friend of Baruch, who reassures her that they are here to help her. He has noted the blood on her throat, and Golda explains what happened. "Why have you come now?" she asks.

Sieger explains that Baruch sent a messenger to him during the night. Baruch anticipated that he and the Hahns would not go entirely undetected, and that a threat to Golda was very likely—only Baruch did not think that the intruders would go to Golda in the night. "Now, Golda, you cannot stay here by yourself, so I suggest that you come with me and stay in my house with my family until Baruch comes back. Meanwhile, the constables will keep an eye on your property."

Sieger looks out the window. A man on horseback arrives. Quickly dismounting, he runs to Golda's door, breathless. Sieger recognizes the man and quickly steps into the adjacent room with the constables, leaving the door ajar.

"Hello, Golda, are you all right? Oh, excuse me, I am Ditmar Erlinger, a neighbor of your brother-in-law. When I rose this morning, my wife, Johanna, went to see Esther, as she thought something happened during the night. She said that no one was home. She became a little concerned and suggested that I come and see Baruch to see if he knew something. Is he here?"

Golda is about to speak, when the magistrate steps out from the next room and quickly cuts her off, saying, "Baruch has just gone out for the morning, but thank you for your concern." Erlinger is shocked to see Karl Sieger and three constables with him. Erlinger does not ask why they are there—he knows, or at least he *thinks* he knows. And Sieger has a very good idea why Erlinger is there. Erlinger bows to exit the room but cannot help but comment on

Golda's injury. "Nasty little cut you have there, Mrs. Goldstein," he says, and leaves quickly. He hopes that his display of concern might work well as a cover for him and allow him further access to Baruch's whereabouts.

Sieger bandages Golda's injury while he instructs the constables to take a few of her basic belongings to the coach. "You will be safe with us," Sieger reassures her. Then they leave, ordering one constable to remain behind.

Chapter 2

The Danger of Security

"As soon as there is life, there is danger." —Emerson

HAVING TRAVELLED 140 KILOMETRES, with a good rest in Heidelberg at Baruch's friend Professor Neumann's house, they arrive in Frankfurt around 8:00 p.m. at 61 Rohrbach Straße, the home of Alexander Hardt, a respected doctor whose house is directly opposite a bakery operated by the Bertram family, who have become good friends and neighbors to Alexander. Ever since he moved here from Offenbach, where his family has lived for many years, Alexander has made himself available to his neighbors in a helpful way. Like the Bertrams, Alexander has many Jewish friends, but strict secrecy surrounds these friendships, as Christian communities do not tolerate Jews. Like animals, they are herded into the Judengasse, in Frankfurt, where most of them live in filth and squalor.

The weary horse stops outside the house, and Alexander rushes out to warmly embrace his friend Baruch and to welcome Baruch's sister and brother-in-law and little Joachim. Alexander takes Joachim in his arms and looks at him tenderly. It brings back memories of his son, Rudolph, when he was a small child. Now he is a big, strong boy of nineteen years. Rudolph comes out of the house to help with the luggage and to help Esther up the four steps. She is feeling feeble and is still in shock.

Itzhak has another coughing attack. "You'd better come inside," says Alexander. "Maybe I can have a look at your chest later."

"Thank you, Dr. Hardt, but no, it is nothing. It is probably this long journey and now the cold night air again."

"As you wish, but keep an eye on it, Itzhak—I know that kind of cough." A house servant prepares to take the coach around the corner to a stable at the rear of Dr. Hardt's home, but Baruch insists that he will accompany him to make sure that the horse and coach are safely shut away.

Alexander's wife, Paula, comes out of the kitchen to greet her guests. "*Herzlich Willkommen—Shalom.*" She speaks quietly to indicate the secrecy that must be maintained. "The evening meal will be ready soon; I've prepared something special for you. Oh—it is kosher," she hastens to add. Even Esther raises a little smile at her hostess's jovial manner.

Joachim is sound asleep in his mother's arms. He did not sleep well on that long journey. For the last hour of the trip, he cried so much that Esther despaired. Itzhak took the child while Esther pulled a pillow over her head and tried to shut her eyes for a little bit. Now, with Esther's permission, Paula takes Joachim and puts him on a little cot in a separate room, where she gently rocks him to sleep with a soothing lullaby. "I usually play him a lullaby on my violin to get him to sleep," Esther says as Paula re-enters the kitchen. "You have such a sweet voice, Paula, it sounds like a violin." Paula blushes a little at the compliment but accepts it graciously.

Dinner is now ready. Although a Mennonite by faith, Alexander nods to Baruch to say a blessing for the meal. Baruch politely complies. The conversation around the table is fairly subdued. When they finish eating, Esther excuses herself from the table and Paula quickly rises to her feet to lead her to the bedroom. When Paula returns, Rudolph kindly helps her with the chores in the kitchen. When all is finished, Rudolph and Paula also say good night.

THE DANGER OF SECURITY

Then the three men sink into a deep, sombre conversation until midnight.

"The oppression of the Jews by the Protestants and the Catholics is very severe here in Frankfurt, not liberal like in Ludwigsburg," Alexander remarks. "We have to be very careful not to give rise to suspicion that we have Jewish guests."

"But surely you can have guests of any sort in your own house, Alexander, no?" Baruch questions.

"That is so, my friend, so long as they are transient. If they stay for any length of time, they have to go and live in the Judengasse. Yes, Frankfurt tolerates Jews, so long as they are filthy rich, like the Rothschild family, but even they have to live in the Judengasse." Baruch looks a little uneasy and changes the subject to the proposition of emigrating to Russia.

"My relatives in Offenbach," Alexander jumps in, "are also thinking about emigrating to Russia, because it offers great opportunities, and since they are Mennonites, they hope to escape the growing persecution of them in Offenbach."

"You see, Itzhak," says Baruch, "many decent people are thinking the same thing."

The next morning, Itzhak and Esther sleep in a little. They wake up as they hear the coach leave the back lane. *Baruch did not say good-bye,* Itzhak thinks, *but then, there was nothing new to talk about. All plans have been carefully laid out.*

"Will Baruch return here with Golda?" asks Esther, yawning and still feeling sleepy.

"Oh, yes, Esther. Your brother is a good man and a man of his word. He has a way with people and very good connections in the upper, social echelons of the city. He will be back here with us in two weeks—no doubt about that."

Just as Joachim stirs, Paula's voice floats up to their bedroom: "*Früstück is fertig!*"

That well-known German signal that breakfast is ready is music to a big, hungry man. There is a measure of anticipation in their voices when they acknowledge Paula's call in stereo "*Wir kommen, wir kommen!*"

Downstairs in the kitchen, the stove is giving off full heat, adding to the room's feeling of security and comfort. "By the way, Itzhak, Baruch left this for you." Alexander motions with his head to a side table, where a parcel is neatly wrapped up with string.

When Itzhak opens it, he can hardly believe his eyes. "That is an immoral amount of money!" he exclaims. "Why did he do that?" Esther just stands there with her mouth wide open. Itzhak's big hands tremble as he holds this huge amount of cash, while he keeps saying, "Why? Why? Why?" as if searching for a rational answer.

Alexander, too, tries to reason with Itzhak. "You yourself said that Baruch is a good man—"

"Yes, but—" Itzhak attempts to interrupt.

Alexander continues, "He obviously feels for you, Esther, and Joachim, and does not want you to starve."

"Starve? *Starve?*" Itzhak jumps up and shakes the parcel of money. "This amount can feed the city of Frankfurt for months!" he retorts.

"Be gracious, Itzhak. You are a fine craftsman. You can set up for yourself another workshop somewhere—maybe in Russia—and raise your family there. Is that not what Baruch wants for you?"

Itzhak slumps back into his chair. "I suppose so...yes...maybe." He is still searching for reasons. Then, with a smile coming over his face, he says, "All right, let's start a new life. We'll start here in Frankfurt, and for you, our dear new friend Dr. Hardt, here is some of that money for you."

"Oh, no, no!"Alexander waves his hands vigorously. "There is no need for that. I am happy to have you as my guests until Baruch returns; besides, Baruch also left me a little parcel to cover the expenses for us all until he comes back." Alexander lifts his package and taps it a few times against his left hand with satisfaction before he slips it into his pocket.

After a hearty breakfast, Itzhak asks Alexander about Baruch's hurried departure. "Before returning home," Alexander starts, "Baruch said he needed to visit a banker in Frankfurt by the name of Rothschild. He had some business to complete with him for the chief magistrate of Ludwigsburg."

"Rothschild?" Itzhak searches his memory. "He came to Ludwigsburg not so long ago. He visited with the chief magistrate." He clicks his fingers to recall the name. "Ah, yes, it was Sieger. Baruch mentioned his name."

Baruch's return trip to Ludwigsburg is rather leisurely and takes over a week. He conducts quite a bit of business on the way home and is most pleased with the results. When he arrives in Ludwigsburg, rather than going straight to his own home, Baruch heads straight for the chief magistrate's house.

Golda comes rushing out to embrace Baruch, and each is surprised to see the other there. When Baruch sees the bandage on Golda's neck, she says, "It's nothing—Karl will explain it to you inside."

Baruch feels a little awkward that Golda is here, but he tries to be nonchalant about it. Once they are inside, the atmosphere rapidly becomes congenial. The magistrate's wife takes Golda to prepare the evening meal. "We'll leave the men to talk," she says taking Golda gently by the arm.

Karl Sieger now relates the incident at Golda's house and apologizes that he did not go earlier to prevent the trauma inflicted on Golda. Baruch is grateful that Karl took her back to a safe place. However, Sieger does not relate to Baruch that he received a messenger from Rothschild the day before. Rothschild wondered when the rest of the money would be delivered, as the amount Baruch delivered was well short of the stipulated amount. Instead, he simply goes on to say, with a little questioning tone in his voice, "Erlinger and his men are onto something. I assume from their anger that they did not catch you with all that money and jewellery for Rothschild?"

"All is fine. Erlinger followed us for a while, but we managed to hide until they left. Rothschild was delighted to see all that money and the loot. However, it appears Erlinger went straight to Golda in his rage over losing that money because of his stupidity. That is something neither of us expected."

"Baruch, we have to be extremely careful now about the way we conduct our business," Karl said, laying one hand on Baruch's shoulder. "People are starting to question our 'business' arrangements. We had to divert their attention to the Jews. Nothing personal, Baruch, you understand. But one Jew had to be the scapegoat, without any physical harm to him. My idea to safely plant some incriminating evidence in your brother-in-law's workshop, send it up in smoke, and let the police find the papers will certainly make it appear that Itzhak tried to burn the evidence with his shop. A brilliant idea, if I say so myself. I was pleased that you eventually agreed to it and cooperated," he said menacingly, staring into Baruch's eyes. "We, I mean you, would not want our little secrets to fall into Erlinger's hands, now, would you?"

"I agree, Karl—Itzhak would have discovered our 'business' sooner or later, and you know how honest and up front he is."

"So it was good you 'persuaded' him to move to Frankfurt and to make it look as if he fled," says Karl. Then, in a questioning tone, "Did you reward Itzhak handsomely? Hmm?"

"Yes, he will be comfortable, Karl."

"So from now on, Baruch, you must follow my orders implicitly and not do anything rash or foolish; otherwise, we will both hang from the gallows—like Oppenheimer, your former colleague. The people are in the mood for this—don't forget it."

"Of course—you are absolutely right, Karl." Baruch hands him a compendium containing a number of documents.

Sieger opens it and peruses the documents with a satisfied look. "Well done, Baruch! Well done!" he says as he closes the compendium.

After a lavish evening meal and good wine, Baruch and Golda say good night. "One more celebratory drink, Baruch," says Karl, who disappears in the drawing room, where he elegantly fills four glasses of fine cognac. With an enthusiastic "*Prost*!" they down the cognac and take off in their coach for home.

"Good evening, Mr and Mrs. Goldstein." The constable who has been guarding the house greets them warmly. "I hope you had a pleasant journey, sir—may I help you with your luggage?" "Oh—you're most kind. Thank you. I'm feeling a bit tired." Golda heads straight up the stairs to her bedroom. Baruch squeezes two gold coins into the constable's hand and bids him good night. Baruch feels unusually tired as well. He barely manages to crawl up the stairs, and passes out near the bedroom door. Golda is already asleep in bed.

Down the street, the constable passes a man. They do not look at each other, say anything, or stop. The constable simply holds out his hand to the stranger, and some exchange takes place between the men. Then both disappear into the dark night in opposite directions.

The scene presents a gruesome sight. The shocked senior policemen stand over two mutilated bodies. Their throats are cut, and the male victim's right hand is cut off. Police say it was a calculated, professional execution. The coroner estimates that the bodies have been here for four days. The house is totally ransacked. The intruders seemed to have meticulously checked every piece of written paper. There are no valuables left in the house of a man who had many. On the wall is written, in blood: *Remember Jud Süß!*

Erlinger and his wife, Johanna, attend the funeral, as does Karl Sieger, who makes a measured show of grief. He secured all the legal documents pertaining to the properties of Baruch Goldstein and Itzhak Hahn, as Baruch previously arranged for Siegers to have power of attorney; all of which is contained in the compendium he was handed by Baruch. Now that Baruch is dead without an heir, and Sieger knows that Itzhak will never come back here again, so, as far as he is concerned, he vanished without a trace, and he has the power and the opportunity to arrange the documents for his own benefit. He orchestrates the whole deal perfectly, selling everything for a handsome sum of money that makes Sieger's bank holdings with Rothschild, in Frankfurt, look good. Sieger laughs, "And I did not have to lift a finger. Even Erlinger removed Baruch for me without my prompting. Marvellous!" He claps his hands. Yet if ever the police find the murderer—Erlinger—Sieger is ready and willing to send him to the gallows.

Following a calculated, deliberate delay, the news finally reaches Itzhak and Esther two weeks later. Esther is inconsolable, and Itzhak bewails his beloved and generous brother-in-law, who came to such a gruesome end with his wife. Dr. Hardt and his wife try to provide some solace but are a little awkward, as they do not understand the Jewish faith well.

That night, while Itzhak and Esther are in bed, he opens his heart and says to Esther, "What right does a human have to play God and determine that another human must die? Why? *Why?*"

Itzhak repeats. "I am losing faith in God and trust in humans, Esther."

"From now on," Esther replies, "we have to be extremely careful, I fear for our lives." They lie there in stunned silence. Now, all their ties with Ludwigsburg are permanently and irretrievably severed. To return and salvage what is left would be suicidal. Now Frankfurt will have to be home for them—or will it?

Chapter 3

The Frankfurter Judengasse

"There's small choice in rotten apples." —Shakespeare

A RAPPING ON THE DOOR EARLY ONE MORNING WAKES ALL IN THE HARDTS' HOUSEHOLD. Alexander opens the door. Two men are speaking seriously to Alexander. As they leave, Itzhak overhears the last thing they say. "Dr. Hardt, you have one week to sort this out. We will be back to ensure you comply with the church and city regulations." The church men have been made aware that Dr. Hardt has Jewish guests, something about which he has been warned previously when he had Jewish visitors. Alexander returns stern-faced to all who by now have gathered in the kitchen. There is no need for anyone to say a word. Everyone knows the reason for the callers, and the consequences of forceful removal of the Hahns to the Judengasse and a boycotting of Dr. Hardt's medical practice.

The day is filled with much anxious conversations and various contingency plans to avoid upsetting the church men even more. Itzhak and Esther feel embarrassed that their visit has put Dr. Hardt in such an awkward position. Still Dr. Hardt is reassuring them that he has all under control. Esther is concerned for Itzhak. He looks a little pale and seems weak. During the night, Itzhak has a major coughing fit and starts to cough up blood. This frightens Esther, who rises from her bed and gently knocks on the bedroom door of Dr. Hardt, who is already up and dressing himself. Itzhak lies in bed in a pool of sweat and very short of breath. Esther kneels beside the bed and holds Itzhak's large hand. Dr. Hardt examines the color of the blood-tinged sputum. He then listens intently to Itzhak's breathing and heartbeat. Dr. Hardt looks at Esther with compassion and says: "The shock of the fire and now the murder of Baruch and Golda exacerbated his condition. He will need a lot of rest for a very, very long time. You are welcome to stay here until we can work out something more permanent. I will talk to the church men to assure them that this is an emergency but definitely temporary."

Paula is already in the kitchen; Alexander told her to go and make hot chicken broth even before Esther knocked on the door. The three of them help Itzhak sit up in bed and drink the broth. He is feeling very weak. Dr. Hardt is certain that it is consumption (pulmonary tuberculosis) but is not ready yet to tell Itzhak or Esther. He gives Itzhak some cod-liver oil to ease the coughing. Itzhak's breathing is now easier. When he recovers a bit he thanks Dr. Hardt for his kindness and hopes he has not inconvenienced him by this. They all then return to go to sleep. For Esther however this is not possible. She lays awake listening to Itzhak's breathing.

Alexander is up early the next morning to see how Itzhak is doing. He finds some Cinnamic acid in his medical supplies and prescribes it to be taken parenchymatously. Esther looks a little confused when she hears this instruction. Realizing that she does not understand, says, "Oh that means to be taken orally— by mouth." Esther nods.

Alexander then explains the serious nature of the illness to both Esther and Itzhak. He will have to be isolated for some months, if not years, in a sanatorium that Dr. Hardt founded with his colleagues, which is farther north of Frankfurt in Bad Homburg. "We have to act quickly. This will be his best chance to survive and stop the infection from spreading to others in the house. Do you know, Esther, what that means for you and Joachim?"

Esther nods. She knows the implications and asks Dr. Hardt to take care of the finances and to use their newly acquired monies to pay for their needs. She trusts him implicitly. Although she would manage her finances extremely well, she thinks it best to leave the money with Dr. Hardt, where it may be safer, since any disclosure of the fact that she is quite well off may make her a target of unscrupulous men.

The next day, Alexander takes Itzhak to the sanatorium in his coach. A tearful Esther says good-bye to her husband. Perhaps she will never see him again. Life is now on the knife's edge. The only certainty in a bewildering array of uncertainties is that Esther will have to live in the Judengasse. For how long? That is yet another unknown.

※

Four days later, Dr. Hardt delivers Esther and Joachim to the house of Rothschild, whose name means "Red Shield," and lives in a very nice house called "Zum Grünen Schild," meaning "At the Green Shield," in the Judengasse. He financed practically all the buildings in the street. Rothschild shows Esther and Joachim the small unit, up two sets of stairs, at the far end of the Wollgraben, the proper name of the street, which is closed off with a gate from the other street called Fischerfeld Straße. Another two gates, strategically placed, complete the ghetto. Rothschild informs Esther of all the curfew restrictions, which include the locking of the gates at dusk, on Christian Holy Days, or when nobility comes riding into town. No Jews are to be seen on the streets of Frankfurt during these curfews. "Incidentally," says Rothschild sarcastically, "for the privilege of being locked up in this 'cage,' we all have to pay the Christians to do that for us. There is a tax that each one of us has to pay for this, to show our deep appreciation for their services."

"What if we need urgent help during curfews?" Esther looks at Rothschild with deep concern.

"Just make sure you have no 'emergencies'—otherwise, you will have to rely on those here in the ghetto."

Many buildings in this section still have the charred timbers of the 1721 fires that ravaged the Judengasse. Those houses that were completely destroyed have been rebuilt in even more cramped spaces to accommodate the rapidly growing numbers of Jewish residents. Houses that survived were roughly repaired and modified to take in more arrivals. Dr. Hardt has already arranged payment for the unit, in accordance with Esther's wishes. What meets Esther's eyes, ears, and nose brings on an attack of nausea. Most of the buildings have no toilets, and often the excrement is thrown out of the windows onto the narrow street below. Those with toilets send it via a chute into the moat behind the city wall. The stink is unbearable. The crowded conditions are a hotbed of infectious diseases, as well as a source of constant bickering and fighting among the oppressed poor. This is exacerbated by the fact that most Jews do not leave the ghetto more than once a year. Some ten thousand people are crowded in this single, curved street, 330 meters long and three to four meters wide, that was originally allocated for twenty-some families. Looking up, Esther sees a mass of countless heads poking out of windows, all seemingly wanting to grab a lungful of fresh air. The streets are littered with children, and steps to the houses are barely visible because so many people are sitting on them.

After Rothschild leaves her, she stands in front of the door of her unit and cries. A gentle hand touches her shoulder. "Shalom—welcome. My name is Isabella Schnapper. I live also in the Judengasse with my family. There are a lot of my relatives living here. We know this is not a good place for us to live, but we have no choice, as you well know. Yet we help each other to make the best of life here. I want to help you also."

Such kind words coming from someone whose facial expressions are as deserted of expression as a scorched wilderness take Esther by surprise. "Thank you, Isabella. I will need all the help I can get to settle in this godforsaken street. My name is Esther, and this is my son, Joachim."

"And no husband?" asks Isabella.

"Come inside, Isabella; then I will tell you about my husband."

Esther enters the unit and stops suddenly, stunned, while Isabella stands behind her. There are a table and chairs and beds, beautifully made up, and a kitchen supplied with crockery and utensils. The table is decked with a prettily embroidered cloth; on it are set a few basic food items and some fruit. "It is nice, isn't it, Esther?" says the voice behind her. Esther turns around and sees Isabella smile and is about to thank her.

"No—don't thank me. Dr. Hardt came here yesterday and had this all set up for you. Very nice man…Is he…is he…your…lover?"

"Isabella!" says Esther, quite outraged.

"Oh, I'm sorry, I meant no offense," Isabella apologizes. "I just—"

"No." Esther stops her emphatically. "Let me put Joachim in his new cot, and then I will tell you all about my husband, Itzhak, and Dr. Hardt."

Before Isabella leaves to return to her own family, she asks, "How will you support yourself, Esther?"

"Herr Rothschild asked me to do his bookkeeping. I was brought up in a banking family, and I also teach violin to the Rothschild children. I can keep Joachim with me where I work."

"Oh, Esther, that is just wonderful." The women hug each other, and Isabella disappears in the herd of people outside.

Over the ensuing months, a bond of friendship begins to build between the two women.

The years pass with only a few messages about Itzhak from Dr. Hardt and the occasional visits he arranges for her to see Itzhak. Since her visit to Itzhak in the sanatorium last autumn, she worries, as he seems to be getting weaker. Working for Rothschild is a blessing, not only because it keeps her occupied, but also because it allows her to save a nice amount of money. Joachim and Esther survive yet another bad influenza epidemic that sweeps through Frankfurt and has a particularly devastating effect on the population in the Judengasse. Several of the Schnapper children die, and Isabella herself falls victim to the epidemic. The steady flow of carts with little and large coffins taken to the Jewish cemetery is a sight that breaks even the toughest of Jewish hearts. But nothing is as heart-wrenching as seeing the coffin of a mother and her child taken away together.

The summer of 1745 passes; Joachim is three years old. There is high excitement in Frankfurt in preparation for the coronation ceremony of Francis I, emperor of the Holy Roman-German Empire. Frankfurt has been the coronation city for the emperors of the Holy Roman-German emperors for a considerable time, and the tradition continues. This coronation for Francis I will take place on Friday, October 4.

Wednesday morning arrives, and all the Jews are to be locked in the Judengasse. The parish officers arrive at 7:00 a.m. to lock the Wollgraben gate, just as Dr. Hardt arrives to give Esther a message. The parish officers deny him access. He calls to a man near the gate to ask if he can find Esther Hahn, who lives near the gate. Esther just happens to look out of the window to watch the closing of the gates. She recognizes Dr. Hardt, and, after checking that Joachim is still asleep, runs down to the gate. Dr. Hardt, believing that Esther is not to be found, is about to get into his coach, when she arrives at the gate. "Dr. Hardt! Dr. Hardt!" she calls, using all the strength in her voice to make it rise above the constant din in the Judengasse.

With one foot on the tread board of the coach, he stops and turns his head. He sees Esther, stops, and then walks very slowly toward her with his head bowed. As he comes closer to the gate, he lifts his hat and looks Esther in the eye for a moment without

The Frankfurter Judengasse

speaking. A frightened look comes over Esther's face, and Dr. Hardt's eyes begin brimming with tears. He sinks to his knees and says; "We did all that could be done for Itzhak. He was very brave. He asked me to give you this letter, which he dictated to me to write, as he was too weak to do it himself."

Reluctantly, Esther holds out her trembling hand to accept the envelope and then suddenly grabs it and thrusts it against her bosom with the same force a desperate person would use to plunge a knife into their heart to end the pain and misery of this life. She turns and runs back to her house.

"Esther, please!" Dr. Hardt calls after her, But Esther does not respond. Dejected, Dr. Hardt enters into his coach and slowly, very slowly, makes his way home to 61 Rohrbach Straße.

Esther falls on her knees next to the bed where Joachim sleeps. She lets out a heart-rending groan that wakes Joachim, who looks bewilderedly at his mother. He does not ask what is wrong, but hugs his mother as she breaks down in tears. Joachim rises a little while later and finds some bread and milk in the kitchen for his breakfast. Esther has prepared her son for this possible eventuality that Papa my not come back to them again. Then she would hug him and cry. She explained what death is, since Joachim has lost some of his friends in the Influenza epidemic. Thus, when Esther returns to the kitchen, Joachim looks at his mother and says, "Has Papa died?"

She nods her head and once again bursts into tears. "Joachim, my sweet little boy, can you get dressed and run over to Mr. Rothschild and tell him that I am not well enough to come and work today?" she says between heavy sobs.

A few minutes later, Mr. and Mrs. Rothschild stand at her door with little Joachim. She invites them into her humble home. They all sit silently around the table for quite a while. Mr. Rothschild sees the unopened, tear-stained letter on the table. "Can you not bring yourself to read it?" Rothschild asks, pointing to the letter. Esther shakes her head. "Would you like me to read it to you?"

Esther looks at him with her eyes swimming in tears. She says nothing for a while, and then she nods her head, as if she has summoned up enough courage to hear it.

"Are you quite sure you are ready for it?" asks Rothschild in a fatherly voice. She again nods emphatically. Rothschild opens the letter, notes the date—"Bad Homburg, September 30, 1745"—and begins to read:

"My dearest Esther and Joachim; shalom and shalom! May you have peace and prosperity. By the time you get this letter, I, too, will be at peace. Today, I have no more pain and a great calmness has come to my troubled soul. A little while ago, I was angry with God and angry with the Christians who have inflicted so much pain on us. Now I am no longer angry with God. Alexander has explained to me that the God of the Bible is not responsible for all the suffering and pain. It is caused by those who claim to be Christians but who do not act in Christian ways. I forgive them totally. As Alexander read me some passages from the Bible about a future life that we may have in the resurrection, in the paradise here on Earth, a ray of hope has lit up my darkened heart. Oh, my dear Esther, the only pain I have is from my desire to hold you once more in my arms and to kiss you and Joachim."

Esther can no longer endure it. In a burst of unspeakable pain, her head drops onto the table and she sobs uncontrollably. Rothschild folds the first page of the letter and decides not to read the next page. He puts the pages back into the envelope and lays it next to Esther's hand. "You can read the rest later," he says. He stands up and leans over Esther and kisses her head. He whispers to his wife to stay there and look after them. Then he exits quietly.

✦

The coronation of Francis I comes and goes with much pomp and ceremony, yet the gates to the Judengasse remain closed until

Monday morning. The Sabbath will run until 6:00 p.m., but then the gates will have to be locked for the night curfew, and Sunday is the Holy Day for the Christians. This long curfew over five days starts to irritate the residents of the Judengasse, and some become quite vocal about it.

Mrs. Rothschild pays much attention to Esther over this period, bringing her food and spending time with her. She also takes Joachim to play with her children. This allows Esther the time to meditate and deal with her grief. As she meditates, she involuntarily recalls a very sad piece of music. In her head she hears the violin play. It becomes stronger and stronger, as if a great power wants to vanquish her and her grief wants to swallow her up. She has a sudden compulsion to grab the violin and play this music, as if it is the only escape from this inevitable journey into a depressive oblivion.

The din on the staircase stops as the music flows out to the people there. She plays this F-sharp-minor piece with such intensity that it not only grips the strings of her violin with great passion but also pulls the strings of her heart. Behind her door, she hears the quiet wailing of women who are touched by the music. When Esther finishes, a great sense of relief comes over her. She is released from the terror of despair.

She wonders what Dr. Hardt has arranged for the funeral. Then she remembers the letter. She opens it, scans the first page, and then begins to read the second page, which continues:

Please try and find some happiness in your life. Take Joachim to Russia, as we had planned to do together. I have spoken with Alexander in great detail about this. He will arrange everything for you. There will be difficulties ahead for you, but I know you are a very strong and discreet woman.

My heart keeps failing me, and it will soon stop, but my love for you will not. It is as strong as when we were married a few short years ago. Oh, how much joy we had. Thank you for all the happiness you have shared with me, your laughter, your smile, and your music. Please teach Joachim to play the violin. Find him a good master to teach him the trade of his father, as I would have done, in the best tradition of our Jewish heritage.

Shortly I must be gathered to my ancestors. Bless you, my dear Esther, bless you. Praise Jah, for his loving kindness is to time indefinite.

I love you.

Itzhak

❖

The funeral for Itzhak is a miserable affair. The cold autumn wind sends a chill through Esther's soul. She holds on tightly to Joachim. The rain drizzles steadily, and the rabbi's speech is short and quite forgettable. In attendance are Dr. Hardt and his wife, Paula, and Mr. and Mrs. Rothschild. After paying their condolences to Esther and thanking the rabbi, the Rothschilds leave. Dr. Hardt and Paula take Esther and Joachim back to 61 Rohrbach Straße for some refreshments, to warm themselves for a while, and to just sit and talk, after which they take them back to the Judengasse.

Over the ensuing years, Esther thinks much about Russia and what kind of life may lie ahead of them if they can get out of this hellhole. Little pieces of news come to Esther via Rothschild or Dr. Hardt. Esther is particularly impressed with the academic and musical advancements in Russia; they inspire her to keep practicing her violin.

The winter of 1755 is particularly cold. Esther passes the time working for Rothschild and teaching the violin to the more well-to-do Jews in the Judengasse. Joachim is growing rapidly and has broad shoulders, like his father. He is also beginning to learn the violin. Dr. Hardt was able to purchase a violin that suits Joachim perfectly. Esther, herself a well-educated woman, fears for Joachim's development in this mentally depressive environment, devoid of intellectual stimuli. Esther always uses the "locked-up days" to teach Joachim the violin, French, German, Hebrew, Russian and mathematics. Mathematics comes as naturally as breathing to Joachim. The carpenter and cooper Aaron Schnapper has taken Joachim on to work with him and to teach him the basic skills of working with wood, something that gladdens Esther's heart.

December 10, 1755, is deeply etched in Esther's memory. Esther and Joachim arrive early at the Rothschild's house; the servant girl takes Joachim inside and informs Esther that her work is laid out on the desk. The Rothschilds left for Ludwigsburg earlier and will not be back for quite a few days. Esther begins her routine work with keeping ledgers and filing mail. Among the letters to be filed is one from Mr. Sieger, chief magistrate of Ludwigsburg. Esther instantly has a bad feeling about this letter. Against her better judgment, she reads it before filing it away.

Dear Mr. Rothschild,
The unfortunate incident of the missing money that was to be conveyed to you by Mr. Goldstein in February 1743 has now been resolved to our mutual satisfaction. It appears that Mr. Goldstein somehow misappropriated large sums of that money, owing to you, while he was in Ludwigsburg. However, proceeds from the sale of his property and goods are now in my safekeeping. It appears from your letters that the amount of 25,000 gulden was missing. This amount of money plus interest is here for your collection. This should settle matters between us nicely. I await your visit in due course.
Your obedient servant,
Karl Sieger

For a moment Esther is frozen at the desk. As the maid enters to offer some refreshments, Esther gathers her composure and takes the food, but her mind is racing furiously. *That was exactly 20,000 gulden that my brother, Baruch, left with us, and 5,000 for Dr. Hardt. Is Rothschild aware that I now have that money? Was he behind the murder of my brother?* She searches frantically for further correspondence from Sieger and finally comes upon a letter from Sieger dated March 15, 1743, in which Sieger emphatically exonerates Itzhak and Esther Hahn of any involvement in the fraud. "So it is neither Sieger nor Rothschild who murdered my brother, and that leaves Erlinger," she whispers to herself, and gives a deep sigh of relief. "Then it must have been Erlinger's money that Baruch carried in the coach, and that is why he pursued us the night we left Ludwigsburg, and I now have that money!"

Inside Esther is growing a dreadful fear, a foreboding sense of an impending disaster that must be avoided at all costs. "If he murdered Baruch and Golda, what is stopping him from finding Joachim and me and killing us as well?" She calls the maid. "When will Mr. and Mrs. Rothschild return?"

"About the end of January, madam; from Ludwigsburg, he will also travel to Stuttgart to visit the Mendelssohns before returning to Frankfurt. Will that be all, madam?"

"Yes, thank you," Esther says. The maid leaves the office.

During the so-called "Christmas" celebrations, the Judengasse is once again closed for almost a week. This leads to much frustration among the more radical members of the Judengasse.

Any sign of even the smallest rebellion is always met with the full force of the church and state. In her fear of Erlinger's possible revenge, Esther feels almost protected by the closure of the Judengasse. However, this uneasiness gives her the determination to escape this hellhole of misery and despair. Immediately, she writes a letter to Dr. Hardt. A week later, his response arrives.

Dear Esther,

Your fears are not unfounded. A certain Mr. Erlinger from Ludwigsburg came to visit me. His wife, Johanna, is feeling poorly. She appears to have had a nasty accident. She is badly bruised. He says that he is here on a certain business involving the recovery of stolen money. I am just so grateful that you have warned me ahead of his visit, lest I might have opened my mouth too much. As it is, he knows that you and Itzhak visited with me.

He got that information from the church officials who came here that early morning.

Please, Esther, keep a low profile for the next few days and do not unnecessarily go out of your house, as Erlinger will keep a close watch on the Judengasse. Now, please follow my instructions explicitly. I will visit you several times in the next few days in the capacity of a doctor. However, each visit I will take out some of your belongings, which you will have carefully packed. I will ensure that Erlinger, who now knows me, will see me. Each time I will leave by the Wollgraben gate. That is where he will be expecting me. On the fourth day, I will not take anything with me. I will act as a decoy. I will act in a suspicious manner that will alert Erlinger and his henchmen, so he will probably stop me or follow me. You, however, will be leaving with Mr. Aaron Schnapper in his wagon via the gate to the Fischerfeld Straße. All arrangements for your safekeeping have been made. Just follow Mr. Aaron Schnapper's instructions.

Dr. A. Hardt

On the fourth day, before Dr. Hardt says good-bye to Esther, he places a thin leather strap around her neck, on which dangles a small key. "Hide it safely in your bosom; you will know soon enough why you have it." When the coach leaves the Wollgraben gate, a calculated half an hour before the curfew, Erlinger and eight officials jump out from their hiding place and stop the coach in a well-orchestrated interception.

"Good evening, Dr. Hardt," says Erlinger in a sarcastic voice. "I just wanted to let you know that your treatment for my wife has worked a miracle for her recovery. You are such a fine doctor. It is commendable that you are also looking after the Jewish population's health." He nods his head in the direction of the Judengasse.

"Well, thank you for such accolades. Will that be all, then?" Dr. Hardt replies.

"Almost," Erlinger says with an emphatic voice. "You have such a beautiful coach—would you mind if I and these gentlemen had a closer look?"

"You are most welcome, gentlemen." Dr. Hardt lifts his hat and bows to them. "I will be happy to show you every little detail." Dr. Hardt is stalling for time. "I have a box at the rear of the coach. It is perfect for carrying large items." Dr. Hardt laughs. "You could carry an adult body in it. But you gentlemen would not be interested in seeing it—would you?"

"No, no…I mean yes! I am thinking about such a contraption for my own coach." Erlinger looks a little embarrassed but accepts Dr. Hardt's offer to inspect it. Dr. Hardt now pretends he cannot find the key. Finally he opens the box. A large blanket seems to cover a big object. Two officers rip off the blanket, as they are sure that Dr. Hardt is hiding Esther there. They recoil at the sight of a butchered pig. "Not exactly Jewish cuisine," quips Dr. Hardt, with a mischievous smile. "I had to cover it. The Jews would kill me if they knew I had brought a pig into the Judengasse."

The officers slam down the lid and jump off the back of the coach. Straightening up their coats and pulling their sleeves, they cough, highly embarrassed and even a bit offended, that they have been made fools of. "Do you know where Esther Hahn is?" demands Erlinger. All pretense of being polite has vanished.

Dr. Hardt shrugs his shoulders. "Well, the last I saw of her was in her house, a few minutes ago, when I attended to her son. That's where she probably is, for all I know. You'd better go and see for yourself."

The men start running into the Judengasse. Dr. Hardt calls out after them, "Be careful entering the house—the little boy seems to have developed the plague." They stop dead in their tracks. Dr. Hardt waves good-bye as his coach moves on. Erlinger throws his hat to the ground and then kicks it in a fit of rage. The gates begin to close. While Dr. Hardt was "entertaining" Erlinger, Aaron Schnapper timed his departure with Esther and Joachim to perfection.

Chapter 4

The Journey to the Sea

"Give me a light that I may tread safely into the unknown."
—Minnie Louise Haskins

THEY TRAVEL IN THE FADING LIGHT FOR JUST A SHORT DISTANCE OUT OF FRANKFURT. The sunset is particularly beautiful on this winter evening. Esther is wrapped tightly in a blanket, with Joachim close to her. Aaron Schnapper steers his wagon into a farmyard. "We have to stay here in the hay barn for the night. The owner knows we are here. We will be warm and safe here," he says reassuringly to Esther. "At first light there will be a comfortable, modern coach waiting for you. You will get into that coach, and it will take you to Offenbach, to relatives of Dr. Hardt. I will stay here for the night to watch over you, and in any case I cannot return to the Judengasse, as the gates are closed for that damned curfew."

Esther is grateful for this break; she snuggles up to Joachim deep in the hay under a stack of blankets and drops off to sleep. When she wakes up, Aaron Schnapper is gone. A servant girl from the farm appears with a tray holding a freshly baked loaf of bread, some butter and cheese and honey, and two cups of hot rose-hip tea. She places it near them. Esther wants to thank her, but the girl just waves her hand to stop her from saying anything and then disappears.

The shiny black coach is waiting for them outside. On this frosty January 22, a rare clear blue sky has the sun glistening on the snow-covered landscape when Offenbach comes into view. From the window of the coach, it presents a tranquil picture to Esther. A sense of security comes over her. Joachim is asleep with his head on her shoulder. Twenty minutes later, the coach stops in front of a moderately sized house with a garden. Even under the snow cover, she sees that it has been carefully manicured. The footman opens the door and holds out his hand to support Esther as she gets off the coach, careful not to slip on the snow. She then turns to help Joachim, who seems not to have woken fully.

Three men come out of the house. The smallest of the three walks up to Esther and introduces himself. "My name is Rudolph—Rudolph Hardt. You must be Esther Hahn, and this, of course, is Joachim."

Esther nods her head and does a little curtsy. "Mr. Hardt—"

"No, please, Rudolph, or even Rudi," he interjects.

Esther begins again: "Mr. Hardt—I mean, Rudolph—it seems inappropriate, even a little over familiar, to address a man of such great kindness, and who is giving refuge to a wretched person like me, by his first name, but at your bidding, I shall get used to it."

He introduces his house servant Max, a large-framed man much like Itzhak, and his son, Peter, who, after a polite welcome, takes the items from the coach. As they unload, Peter calls his father over to the coach. He points to a small, locked leather travelling case that has written on it: *This case must be carried only by Esther Hahn. Signed, Dr. A. Hardt.* Rudi calls back Esther, who is being welcomed by Anneliese Hardt, Rudolph's wife, and points to the case and its inscription. He asks Esther to lift it up herself. She has been wondering how Dr. Hardt was going to get the money to her. The key to the case is hidden safely in her bosom.

After a refreshing lunch, Rudi, Anneliese, and Peter call Esther into the living room. The house servants entertain Joachim in the kitchen, from which much laughter can be heard. Rudi reveals his conversations with his brother, Alexander, who made all the arrangements for Esther and Joachim to emigrate to Russia. "Everything is paid for the trip up to the Baltic Sea. In Lübeck you will board a ship to St. Petersburg in Russia. You may have to wait a little while in Lübeck before you can arrange a suitable passage to St. Petersburg."

Rudi looks at Esther, who seems overcome with the thought of negotiating her way to Russia alone with her son. Peter sits transfixed, looking at Esther. When Rudi explains the other half of the plan, Esther becomes more cheerful again. "By now, Erlinger and Rothschild will have discovered that you are no longer living in the Judengasse. Rothschild will be disappointed, but Erlinger will be furious. He will go and search for you," Rudi states with a measure of concern.

"Why are you telling me this?" Esther asks.

"To help you understand that you will have to leave here the day after tomorrow. It will be an arduous trip, but with Peter travelling with you, it will all work out well."

❖

Esther is fearful that Erlinger will find her in Offenbach, so it comes as a relief when the day of their departure arrives. Anneliese and Rudi say a tearful good-bye to their thirty-five-year-old son, Peter. "Don't forget to write, Peter," his mother calls out to him.

Soon the stagecoach disappears in the glistening morning sun, which provides at least a little cheer, and heads in a north-easterly direction toward Hannover, a distance of 260 kilometres. Peter calculates that if the horses can travel ten or more kilometres per hour, it will take two days to get there with an overnight stop at Fulda and changing the team of horses. They will then travel to Hannover the next day, with a rest overnight, and then the 150 kilometres to Hamburg, which will get them there in one more day. From Hamburg, the stagecoach will take them the sixty-seven kilometres to Lübeck

Esther is impressed with Peter's mathematical calculations. "I am an architect; mathematics is my bread and butter," Peter says without a hint of pride.

Half a day into the journey, Esther asks Peter, "Why are you doing this for me?"

"Mrs. Hahn—"

"Please, call me Esther."

"Very well, then, Esther, I am doing this for myself. You are my traveling companion—a pretty one at that." He looks at Esther, who blushes a little at this compliment and tries to look the other way. For a moment, Peter just looks at her beautiful shoulder-length, wavy hair, perfectly trimmed and groomed, hugging her pretty face. A neat hat sits like a tiara on her head, giving her the look of a queen. A full, flowing skirt, with a tight-fitting jacket tugging at her small waist, accentuates her feminine figure. He is silent for a moment longer, before he answers, "I am very happy that this arrangement coincides with mine, though I had to rush mine along a little. Please, Esther, you are not a burden to me. I'll gladly step in where I can help you without taking charge of everything. You are a bright woman and a talented one as well."

Esther blushes a little more. "Thank you, Peter. I do appreciate what you have done—in fact, what the whole Hardt family has done—for me and for Itzhak when he was alive. I hope that someday I can repay your kindness."

"No, no, Esther, you do not owe me a thing. I think we shall just be good travelling companions. All right?"

"All right, then!" Esther smiles and nods her head.

"What will you do in Russia, Esther—I mean, how will you support yourself? You cannot rely on your..." He nods with his head to Esther's leather case.

"I will apply for a position in the St. Petersburg orchestra and teach the violin privately or at the music academy. There is much work to be had in the culturally thriving city of St. Petersburg, I hear. I can also do bookkeeping as a job, as I did for Rothschild in Frankfurt."

"Rothschild? Mmm, that should be a good reference for you," says Peter admiringly.

"And you, Peter? What will you do?"

"I am an architect. I will probably work in this capacity for a while. At heart I am a *Handwerker* [a tradesman who works with his hands]. Before my father made me study architecture in Heidelberg, I did my apprenticeship as a blacksmith in Offenbach. I loved that physical work. So, I do not see my life steeped in Russian culture and snobbery. As an architect I can make good money, but if the opportunity arises, I want to live in the country. Eventually I will probably set up a forge and work as a blacksmith. Shoeing horses, making tools and plows—there will always be work for me." Peter touches Esther's hand gently.

Esther is startled and pulls her hand away quickly. She stares at Peter. "Oh, Peter! Please! I am a widow…I…Besides; we hardly know each other…You must not play with my feelings…We…You…" Words fail to come to her bewildered mind.

"I am deeply sorry, Esther; it was meant as a gesture of friendship, nothing more."

"I am sorry too, Peter. Everything is still so raw inside me. I hardly know who I am at the moment. Can you understand that, Peter?" She looks at him questioningly with eyes that glisten like two large black pearls.

This time, he pats her hand firmly, and with a smile he says, "Sure, Esther, I can and I do understand. Everything will be fine. Trust me."

"Yes, of course, everything will be fine," she repeats in an acquiescent tone. A moment of silence ensues. Then they look at each other with a big smile and burst into laughter. Joachim stirs from his sleep.

"You're a brave woman, Esther, going to a foreign country as a widow with a son. I admire your courage." Peter goes on, "What will Joachim do?"

"I hope I can find someone to tutor him in the Russian language in St. Petersburg, so he can learn to speak, read, and write Russian fluently. My Russian is not that good, but I can get by with it. Maybe Joachim will help me to improve it." Esther stops for a moment and then continues, "His father's wish was that he should be apprenticed to learn the craftsmanship of a coachbuilder, as Itzhak was, or the cooper trade. Kegs are always in demand." Peter laughs. "What is so funny, Peter?" Esther pretends to sound outraged.

"Drinking alcohol and Russians go together like 'horse and cart,' 'needle and thread'…"

"Husband and wife," Esther adds.

"What I am trying to say, Esther, is, might it not be better for him to learn the trade of brewing and making vodka?" Now Peter's eyes are fixed questioningly on Esther.

"I see your point, Peter, but Russia will have enough drunks staggering around St. Petersburg without Joachim's contribution to it." They both laugh out loud again.

"Then I will help you to find the best coachbuilder in St. Petersburg, where he will learn his father's trade."

"Thank you, Peter. I will remind you of that promise if you stay in St. Petersburg, of course…Will you stay, Peter—will you?"

Her question takes Peter by surprise. "I cannot say, Esther—none of us can. What will Russia bring for us? We must wait and see. I should not have made such a rash promise, but God willing, I will keep it—OK?"

"Of course. I must not take advantage of your friendship," Esther says apologetically.

Chapter 5

The Manna

"Pleasures newly found are sweet." —Wordsworth

AFTER FOUR WEARY DAYS OF TRAVELING AND SLEEPING IN GUESTHOUSES IN FULDA, Hannover, and Hamburg on the way, the coach finally reaches its destination of Lübeck. "Uncle Alex has already paid for our stay in Lübeck for as long as it takes for us to secure a passage on a ship to St. Petersburg, so no need to worry. Let's get a good rest tonight, and after breakfast we will give Joachim and ourselves a little treat—Lübecker marzipan!" says Peter. He sounds as if he has just announced the ultimate prize anyone could wish for.

"I have a note here, madam," says the hotel manager to Esther. "It is from Dr. Alexander Hardt. He instructed me to safe keep a certain piece of luggage, which will be locked away in secure storage—may I?" He holds out his hand.

Esther looks at Peter, who nods that he concurs. Esther hands over the locked case. Then they settle into their separate lodgings. As Esther and Joachim drop off into blissful sleep, a sense of security, of being safe from Erlinger's hatred, and of having Peter look after her and her son, falls over Esther like a warm blanket.

After breakfast the next morning, Peter, Joachim, and Esther go sightseeing. The threesome looks at the magnificent Holsten Gate to Lübeck. It is a fitting symbol of the Hanseatic state of the city. Like Hamburg, Lübeck is a story of how freedom can be achieved through banding together trade, commerce, and community. Then there are the huge salt storage buildings. The city just oozes history. *This is a city of trade and wealth,* Esther thinks. There is an air of opulence to some of the buildings and the business houses, and—yes—there are also the marzipan shops. Joachim's eyes widen with delight when he sees all the shapes and sizes of marzipan. There are beautifully colored animal shapes, fruit, flowers, and objects that look real but are made of the most tempting sweet on earth.

Peter takes Joachim by the arm and enters the store. He is agog at the sight that greets his eyes. Such a variety of colored sweets! "Joachim, you may choose one item." He chooses a violin and then hands it over to his mother.

"No, Joachim, that is for you," Esther refuses.

"Mama, this marzipan piece can only be eaten by someone like you—I really want you to have it. Please!" Esther looks again at Peter, who shrugs his shoulders but holds out another two pieces of marzipan, indicating that one is for Joachim and one is for him. Esther smiles and accepts the gift graciously.

Joachim takes a bite out of his apple marzipan and lets out a most delighted "aah." He has never tasted marzipan before. "Come, Mama, eat your violin."

"Oh, I could not destroy something so precious just to satisfy my desire for something I had never tasted before." She looks up to see Peter's eyes fastened onto hers.

"You are correct, Esther. Never destroy anything that is precious to you just to satisfy a craving for something new. But when you are ready for it, you will eat it, won't you?"

Esther is a little embarrassed by the profoundness of what she has just said, which was not lost on Peter. "Yes, of course I will eat it—someday I will."

There are no ships leaving for St. Petersburg, or, for that matter, anywhere. The Baltic Sea, with all that ice floating on it, is too treacherous to navigate in the winter months. The first available ships will leave Lübeck in early March. "That is some six weeks yet," exclaims Esther, "We cannot ask your uncle Alexander to pay for this!"

"My dear Esther, my uncle Alex let me in on a little secret. You will understand what I am saying. Your brother—his name was Baruch?"

"Yes, it was Baruch," Esther confirms.

"Your brother, Baruch, gave Uncle Alexander five thousand gulden."

"Yes, I was aware of that."

"You see, Esther, the Hardts do not take advantage of such gifts. That was really your money, and he used it to pay for some of your expenses in Frankfurt, to make your passage to Russia possible, and to allow me to accompany you. You are indeed *my* benefactor." Peter bows slightly to Esther, who is speechless.

In a few days, they have thoroughly inspected and observed Lübeck's daily life. They explore strange-looking passageways that seem to go through the middle of a house, only to find whole streets of smaller houses behind them that do not match the opulent house at the front. *Perhaps they belong to the poorer workers of the city*, Esther thinks. For some reason, Lübeck inspires Esther. She keeps looking at her marzipan violin and recalling Peter's comments. It gives her a new lease on life.,

"Can we go to a fine-paper merchant, Peter?" she asks him. "I want to buy some music manuscript paper. I feel the need to compose a piece of music that is stirring in my soul. If I don't write it, my heart shall burst."

"Well, that sounds positively serious. Yes, let's go and do it."

In her room, Esther looks at the vanishing winter scenes and begins her composition. "Sonata No. 1 for Violin and Pianoforte, composed by Esther Hahn" is the heading. It looks proud and bold on the first page. She begins to write. One moment the music in her heart is so bold and heroic, if not defiant, that it screams to be released; then it drops into an abyss that drags mercilessly on the heartstrings as if it wants to devour her inner being. She becomes preoccupied with this work, and Peter recognizes her need for privacy. So he takes Joachim, out for a walk every day and to check with the shipowners about booking a passage. Occasionally they hear Esther play bits of her piece on her violin. What Peter hears moves him deeply.

◈

On Tuesday, March 7, Joachim is fourteen years old. Peter wants to buy Joachim something for his birthday but remembers that Esther told him they do not celebrate birthdays. After they have been to the pier and the shipowners' offices, Peter and Joachim come excitedly to Esther's lodgings with the news that they have secured a passage to St. Petersburg, sailing from Lübeck on Wednesday the eighth. There are over two hundred people wanting to book a voyage to Russia on a Russian pink called *Slon* (the Russian word for "elephant"). It has the capacity to carry about 280 passengers. All want to go to Russia, some temporarily, for business reasons, some to make Russia their permanent home.

"We have only today and Tuesday to get ready, because we need to be onboard by nine a.m. on Wednesday," Peter says. "Are you not excited, Esther?" he asks.

"I am, Peter, I am. But I am also scared to face the uncertain future and leave all that is dear to me behind." Esther looks a little melancholy.

"Surely you are not leaving *all* that is dear to you behind," Peter says in a soft tone.

Esther looks at Peter for a moment, then at Joachim, and then says quietly, "No, not all."

Esther carefully packs all her luggage. Her sonata is almost finished. Two violins are securely packed, and so is her marzipan violin. Joachim has come to like Lübeck and its freedom to move about, not like the awful life in the Judengasse.

"Can we not live here, Mama? Do we have to go to Russia? We have enough money to make a comfortable life here," he asserts.

Esther makes Joachim sit down so she can be eye level with him. "My dear, dear Joachim," she says, laying both hands on his broad shoulders, "how I wish for a carefree life for you in a place where we are safe. Lübeck is beautiful, but we are not safe here. You already know too much of what has happened to us Jews. You have seen too much treachery and deception for your young years. One day you will understand that. We are living among 'wolves' here in Germany. Not real wolves, but some very bad people who want to hurt us. Often we don't know who or where they are. We always have to be very careful—all right?" Joachim nods. "Good man. Now, let's finish our packing."

On Tuesday, Esther goes to the safe at the hotel, takes 2,000 gulden from the case, and puts the rest back in the safe after locking the case. She hands the money to Peter and Joachim to go and pay the shipowners the fee for the three of them. After Peter's return, they take one more stroll through the shops of Lübeck, and Joachim treats Peter and his mother to a piece of marzipan from his own pocket money. "Oh, this is so lovely," says Joachim.

"No wonder you don't want to leave Lübeck. Now I know why you want to stay here," his mother quips.

A little embarrassed, Joachim replies, "Oh, Mother, I am not a little child anymore."

Chapter 6

Crossing the Sea

"The distance is nothing; it is only the first step that is difficult."
—Marquise du Deffand

EARLY ON WEDNESDAY MORNING, Peter knocks on Esther's door. She and Joachim are ready. They collect the case from the hotel, place it safely in Joachim's big hands and, after finalizing matters of payment, head off to the pier where the ship is waiting for them. Already many people are waiting to board the ship. They are businesspeople, intellectuals, and highly skilled craftsmen, most recruited by the Tsarina Elizabeth of Russia.

"Please, let us stay very close together and keep an eye on one another," Peter whispers. Boarding seems slow and tedious, and Esther is becoming nervous. She feels exposed and vulnerable in a crowd like this and automatically grabs Peter's arm. A comfortable warmth flows between them. Finally, they get onboard and put their belongings in storage, except what they have packed separately for their needs during the voyage. Their passports are stamped *Lübeck, March 8, 1756.* Esther deposits her "case" in the ship's safe.

At 9:30 a.m., the ship casts off slowly from the pier, amid turbulent currents from the incoming tide. Most passengers are at the railings, waving good-bye to their homeland. Suddenly someone comes rushing up the pier, screaming and waving his hands. "Where is that bitch? I want to kill her, I want to kill her! Stop the ship!" he shouts, followed by a string of German expletives describing an undesirable character, ranging from a filthy animal to a dirty servant to a loose-living woman. Most people are curious about what this man is doing. As he comes closer, Esther freezes and quickly turns her back and sinks to her knees, while pulling Peter's and Joachim's arms to come down with her. "That is Erlinger!" She can hardly breathe as she says it. Peter and Joachim turn their faces back to Erlinger, knowing that he does not connect them with Esther.

For a moment Erlinger's bloodshot eyes scan the many faces onboard. He is in a blind rage. He is also very drunk and unsteady on his feet. He bends down, and with both hands grabs hold of one of the ropes still dragging on the pier and being hauled onboard, as if to stop the ship from leaving, but it draws him, stumbling, to the edge of the pier. Suddenly, a strong current jerks the ship. Erlinger slips and falls from that forceful pull. He slams his head into a large metal bolt that juts out on a pier support and splits open his head. The people on board scream when they see the blood pouring from his head. He lets go of the rope, staggers to his feet, holds his head with both hands, and then loses consciousness and tumbles into the water. His body disappears quickly under the surging tidal waters, which rapidly take on a red hue. Women are cowering on the deck of the ship, sickened by what they have just witnessed. Some of the pier workers try to rescue him from under the pier but cannot reach him.

Esther does not look to see Erlinger being dragged to his ignominious death. She is trembling at the thought that he might have come aboard to kill her, as well as at the alternative thought that she may have caused a man to die. Peter, who saw everything, is now comforting Esther with his strong arms around her shoulders. "The ship is on its way, Esther. Erlinger will no longer be a threat to you or anyone."

"Those disgusting names he called me, Peter. What will people think of me?" Esther's voice quivers. As the ship gains distance,

CROSSING THE SEA

Peter and Joachim see the lifeless body of a person being dragged out of the water onto the pier. The last things they all see of Lübeck are the many church spires disappearing in the distance as they pass the old lighthouse at Travemünde.

After a little while, Esther rises with the help of Peter's arm. "A lone 'wolf' has perished in his blind pursuit of his prey." Esther speaks with a quiet determination and a sense of finality to a terrifying ordeal. Joachim is pale. His mother had mentioned Erlinger to him from time to time, especially when they escaped the Judengasse.

※

The weather is fine. A gentle breeze is moving the ship under full sail eastward. Still, it is not a fast vessel, and the whole trip may take three weeks or more, depending on the unpredictable spring weather in the Baltic Sea. But that is not all that is uncertain. A couple of days later, Esther stands on the deck, looking out to sea. She senses that she is being watched. *I wonder where Peter and Joachim are,* she thinks. That uneasy feeling intensifies, and she walks off without looking behind her until she is farther away.

When she turns, a woman stares at her. Esther narrows her eyes to see if she can recognize the face. Yes, there is something familiar about her. When she meets up with Peter, she tells him of her strange feelings about that woman. She points in the woman's direction.

"She seems terrified," says Peter. They decide that there is nothing to it, but the following day, Esther once again has a strange feeling of being watched and is equally determined not to look around.

"Esther?" A soft, frightened female voice speaks from directly behind her.

Esther turns and lets out a shriek, which she immediately stifles by covering her mouth with her hand. She stares in disbelief at the woman, whose eyes are filling with tears. "Is that you, Johanna?"

The woman nods, and then lowers her eyes. "Yes, Esther, I am Johanna Erlinger, your neighbor from Ludwigsburg."

"What—what on earth are you doing here on this ship?" Esther manages to ask.

Johanna suddenly rips her scarf off her head and bares her arms. "That is why I am here," she says emphatically. "These bruises and cuts are on my legs and body also."

Suddenly Esther is thrown into confusion. *Is she a friend or a foe?* she thinks. Her eyes dart rapidly from one part of the deck to another, as if to find an enemy hidden somewhere among the people. *Why is Peter not here and where is Joachim?* She is worries.

Johanna notes her bewildered look and covers herself again. "Esther, my dear friend, I am here because of you," she begins. "Do you remember leaving Ludwigsburg that night? You saw me at the window, didn't you? My husband was still asleep, but he woke up when I went back to bed. He asked me why I was up, and I told him a lie. I said I was thirsty and had to take a drink of water from the bedside ewer. About half an hours later, he woke up and went to the window and noticed that Itzhak's house door was left open. The reason I lied was that I knew of some evil plan he made to get even with Baruch over some money and jewels, and knew that if anything went wrong he would kill all of you. Baruch seemed to have involved you and Itzhak in this. I could not bear to see any harm come to you. He ran over and noticed that you had left the city stealthily earlier in the night. He rushed back into our house and ripped the bedcovers off me. He stood there seething with anger. 'Did Baruch Goldstein leave with the Hahns? Speak, you harlot!'

"I cowered on my bed when I received the first blow to my head. As he was about to hit me again, I screamed, 'Stop—I did see Baruch Goldstein and the Hahns leave about two a.m.'

'You bitch,' he screamed, 'you saw them leave and you did not tell me?' He hit me another three times so hard that he broke my nose. He then dressed in a hurry and rode over to his sleazy friend, and they pursued you on the road to Frankfurt, he told me later. On his return, he attacked me again. He was furious to have lost so much money—money he extorted and deposited with Goldstein, as well as a certain amount of jewellery of 'dubious' origin." Johanna pauses.

"So, Erlinger was not after Itzhak and me, but after my brother, Baruch. Did he...Was it he who...?" Esther can barely bring herself to say it.

"Yes, Esther, it was my husband who murdered your brother and his wife." Johanna breaks down and cries. This revelation stuns Esther. "I was beaten again to keep my mouth shut, and again each time he failed to recover his money and jewels. When he threatened to kill me, I simply could not take it anymore. I took eight thousand gulden, and I fled Ludwigsburg and came to Lübeck. I had no choice but to make a new life for myself in a new country."

"So when he ran onto the pier, he wanted to kill you, not me?" Esther questions.

"Yes, it was me he was after. He had no idea, as I had no idea that you were on this ship."

Esther is dumbfounded, but she steps closer to Johanna and hugs her while both cry on each other's shoulder. Esther squeezes Johanna a little harder, out of deep compassion; Johanna instantly flinches a little at this firm touch. Esther lets go immediately and apologizes to Johanna.

"I have three broken ribs, Esther; they are very sore."

Esther kisses Johanna's cheek and says, "You are a true friend to have risked your health and life to protect us. Now we will have to look after each other on this venture."

"Yes, I know," says Johanna. "I have heard of Itzhak's death—I'm so sorry, Esther. But who is that handsome man and the young lad with him? I have seen them with you a lot." Johanna is now a little curious.

"The young lad is Joachim," Esther announces proudly.

"Joachim? Joachim? Oh, my, how he has grown into a beautiful young man. And the man?" She continues her inquiry.

"The man is a relative of Dr. Hardt from Frankfurt."

"Oh - him! I went to him for some treatment while my husband was trying to find out where you are," Johanna says. "He was very, very good. He saw my bruises and pretended to accept my husband's story that I had a dreadful accident. I know he did not believe him, for when I was alone with Dr. Hardt, he said to me, 'Mrs. Erlinger, I know these kinds of "accidents" that wives have. I have seen too many of them. It is strange, you know—it is only the wife that has such terrible "accidents."' But that is enough of my story. Tell me, Esther, what is this handsome man to you?"

"The Hardt family was very good to Itzhak and me, and to Joachim. So when we stayed with his relative in Offenbach, Peter—that's his name, he is Dr. Hardt's nephew—had already made plans to migrate to Russia, so he is here helping me as a travelling companion."

"Please, Esther, would it be too much for me to ask to stay with you and Peter in a group as travelling companions? I have no one, and I feel vulnerable. Please?"

Peter and Joachim have been observing the whole scene from a safe distance, before walking up to the two women.

Esther introduces her companion: "Peter, this is Johanna, my neighbor from Ludwigsburg."

"Johanna Erlinger," says Johanna, holding out her bandaged hand to Peter. Peter is about to shake hands with her, when a jolt of reality hits him and his hand freezes for a second.

"It's all right, Peter," Esther intercedes. "She is also a victim of Erlinger." Johanna and Esther bring Peter up to date on what has happened, and Johanna once again asks if she might be able to travel with Peter, Esther, and Joachim. Peter and Esther accede to her request.

A few days later, as the ship comes within sight of the isle of Rügen, the weather starts to turn stormy. Heavy seas begin washing over the deck. Passengers become seasick, the stench of which overwhelms even the salty smell of the briny sea. Esther, Joachim, and Johanna all feel unwell too. Peter, on the other hand, seems to have quickly gained his sea legs and a good stomach, considering all the vomit around him, so he acts as the nurse for his charges and makes sure they are as comfortable as possible under the circumstances. On a bed not far from where Esther and the others are is a girl about sixteen years old and very sick. Her parents are kneeling next to her bunk and holding her hand. Peter stops and tries to comfort the family. He observes that they are Jewish. "Esther, please, could you go over to that family"—he points— "and share a little comfort with them, since they are also Jews?"

Although still feeling a little feeble from the seasickness, Esther goes over to the family and says "Hello, I am Esther Hahn, and this is my son, Joachim."

"Aaron Stork. My wife, Ruth, and our daughter, Elisabeth," he replies.

"You have such a beautiful daughter." Esther kneels beside the bunk on which Elisabeth lies.

Joachim stands shyly next to his mother and looks at poor Elisabeth. "You will get better soon." He smiles at Elisabeth. "I did."

Turning to Aaron Stork, Esther asks, "Where are you from?"

"Magdeburg, Mrs. Hahn," Aaron Stork replies politely.

"Can we dispense with the formalities, please?" asks Esther. "I am just Esther."

"Fine, we shall address each other by our first names, as friends," Ruth chimes in, and they have a little giggle.

The waters become a bit less disturbed as the ship sails into the narrow passage between the mainland and the southern side of the isle of Rügen, where it anchors at a place called Stralsund to see out the storm. After two more days of raging seas, the sun appears again and all onboard are recovering nicely from their seasickness.

The next day, the ship casts off and continues around the southern tip of the isle before heading out to the deeper parts of the Baltic Sea.

"Mr. Hahn," Aaron says to Peter, "what brings you and your family on this voyage?"

"Oh, I see," says Peter, "I have a bit of explaining to do. My name is Peter Hardt. Esther is not my wife, she is..."

Aaron jumps into a clumsy attempt to save Peter some embarrassment: "No need to explain, Peter, we understand these things."

"No, Aaron, you don't understand. Esther has been recently widowed and only through a family connection, by coincidence, I am travelling with her and Joachim. There is also Johanna, who has joined our group. They need a 'guardian angel,' and that might as well be me."

"Oh, I apologize, Peter—I should be more careful not to jump to conclusions," Aaron pleads.

"Answering your first question, about what brings me on this voyage, I am looking for work as an architect in St. Petersburg," Peter says. "And you, Aaron?"

"I am a goldsmith. In January of this year, I was commissioned by the Tsarina Elisabeth of Russia to do some work on the Amber Room in the Winter Palace. Soldiers are moving it by hand from St. Petersburg to Zarskoje Selo as we speak. Many alterations and additions are planned to blend the Prussian baroque with the Russian rococo arts. They hope to have it finished by 1760, what is referred to as The Eighth Wonder of the World. It is a simply breathtaking piece of art, a treasure beyond price. I will be working on it under the oversight of Bartolomeo Rastrelli, the Italian master."

"What has this to do with the Prussian baroque?" asks Peter curiously."

"I see you don't know the story of the Amber Room," says Aaron. "I have researched it carefully, of course, to fully understand that wonderful piece of art—would you like me to tell you a bit about its history?"

"Oh, I would like it very much," Peter says eagerly, "but would you tell it to all of us? I am sure Esther and Johanna would like to hear it, and I am certain that Joachim might enjoy it. Perhaps we shall all see this Eighth Wonder of the World someday."

When they are all together, Aaron begins his story. "Amber, the 'gold of the Baltic Sea,'" he says, "was and still is a precious commodity. Some folks believe it has magical properties. Around the time of his coronation, the Prussian king Frederick I of Prussia had a grandiose vision of having a room in his castle in Berlin that absolutely no other monarch in Europe has or likely ever will have—a room in which all of the walls are made of amber. Not only for its incredible beauty did he desire this piece of art; he also believed that amber prolongs life. It was so costly to construct the panels for the walls that it almost made Germany bankrupt. Now it was not just amber pieces stuck on a panel—oh no! Each piece of amber was carefully selected and shaped as a piece of mosaic set in gold and jewels to form the most exquisite pictures you could imagine.

"The work was commissioned to a Danish amber cutter named Gottfried Wolffram. This man worked tirelessly for six years, until he was so exhausted that he doubted his ability to finish the work. So, two masters from Danzig, Gottfried Turau and Ernst Schacht, were commissioned to finish the work. They worked for another five years under constant urging from the monarch to hurry and complete the Amber Room. When it was finished, Frederick I, himself a good musician, used it for—, chamber-music performances and receiving writers, philosophers, and poets. Frederick I believed that art and human culture would build and strengthen the state."

"So why is it in Russia now?" asks Johanna, who has considerable experience with jewels and gold.

"Have you ever seen this room, Mr. Stork?" asks Joachim with great curiosity.

"Yes, Joachim." Aaron takes the boy in his arm and gives him a fatherly squeeze. "I have worked on this wonderful piece of art under the guidance of the two masters, for two years. That is why Empress Elisabeth has now asked me to work on this project for her." Joachim is impressed.

"Concerning your question why the Amber Room is now in Russia, could I suggest that we have our evening meal together, and afterward I'll finish telling you the story?" All agree, as their appetite is growing from inhaling the fresh sea air. Joachim catches Elisabeth Stork looking at him with her dark brown eyes.

"When Frederick I died," Aaron continues after their evening meal, "his son Frederick William succeeded him on the throne and was duly coronated in 1713, a year or so after the room was finished. Known as Frederick William I, nicknamed the Soldier King, he had no interest in art and culture. He was a soldier through and through.

"Now, a most incredible thing happened in 1716. Germany was in desperate need of support from the powerful Russian state. So Frederick William I orchestrated a most pompous state reception for Tsar Peter the Great. No other dignitary had ever been received with such pageantry. When Tsar Peter the Great was shown the Amber Room, he was overwhelmed by its glory. It is reported that he said, 'Never have I seen the like!' Wilhelm was pleased with that assessment. But what did he want with such a 'stupid' room, where he could not even "hammer a nail in the wall to hang up his coat?" as he put it. Consequently, he reportedly said, 'In the future, you will always enjoy this view, because I am giving it to you as a symbol of our solid militaristic friendship.'

"Peter the Great accepted this gift graciously. In return he sent fifty-five of his giant soldiers as bodyguards, none shorter than two meters, to the court in Berlin. That worked out to be one soldier per square meter of the Amber Room. The one hundred twenty-five panels of the Amber Room were carefully packed and under military guard shipped to Memel, and then by thirteen sleds to St. Petersburg. There it was partially erected, but now it will come to its glorious completion in Zarskoje Selo, where the palace began to be built three years ago."

◈

When all the others have bunked down, Aaron speaks with Peter on deck under a ship's lantern. "Did you tell me that you are an architect, Peter?"

"Yes, I did. Why do you ask?"

"I know," says Aaron, "that the Empress is looking for several architects to help finish the palace and the Amber Room. I would be pleased to introduce you to her."

Peter is speechless. He was hoping to find any kind of architectural work in St. Petersburg, but this prospect is just too good to be true. "Yes, Aaron, I would be most grateful to you if you could secure some work for me at the palace." Peter's mind is racing with excitement.

The next morning, they all wake up to the sight of the harbor town of Gotenhafen near Danzig The ship is unloading some goods and reloading other merchandise destined for Riga and St. Petersburg. They also replenish their food supplies for the rest of the journey. Passengers are allowed to leave the ship and visit Danzig but are urged to be back before sunset. The ship will sail around nine the next morning.

As they come off the ship, Joachim stays close behind Elisabeth. He is pleased that he does so, because as soon as they step onto the pier, Elisabeth's legs give way under her and Joachim is there to catch her. As he grabs her around her small waist, a warm sensation comes over him. Never has he experienced anything like this.

He played with many girls in the Judengasse, touching them while dancing in the street, but this is different.

"Wow - you are a strong young man," says Elisabeth adoringly, in a way that makes Joachim blush. "Thank you for catching me."

"No need to thank me; it is my pleasure," says Joachim—and he really means it. The Group of Seven, as they now call themselves, takes an open carriage ride to Danzig to see what this ancient city has to offer its visitors. Although the ravages of the Siege of Danzig in 1734 are still visible in parts, the thriving city is full of splendor. They walk along the Royal Way, where the Polish monarchs held their processions whenever they visited Danzig, passing first through the Upland Gate and then through the splendid Golden Gate, which was added to the Royal Walk in 1614. Peter is enraptured when they look at the massive redbrick Gothic architecture of St. Mary's Church, construction on which began in the fourteenth century and took 150 years to complete. It is one of the world's largest churches and can hold up to twenty-five thousand people.

As they stroll through the city, Joachim spots a marzipan shop. He is eager to taste that precious sweet again, but is even more eager to buy a piece for Elisabeth. He enters the shop and lets Elisabeth choose her piece of marzipan. Excitedly he hands it to her and says, "You have never tasted anything like this. Please eat it." She graciously accepts it from Joachim. Elisabeth is more impressed by Joachim's attentiveness than by the marzipan, even though she thinks it exquisite. Joachim, on the other hand, is surprised at how different this marzipan tastes from the kind he had in Lübeck. The German-speaking owner of the shop laughs a little when Joachim mentions it to him.

"My dear boy," he says, "you are tasting the famous Königsberger marzipan. It is quite a different recipe. Don't you like it?"

"Oh, no, sir, I like it very much. It is just different from the Lübecker marzipan; it doesn't seem as sweet," Joachim hastens to add.

On the way back to the ship, Joachim sits next to Elisabeth. The hitherto tongue-tied Joachim becomes quite talkative, much to the surprise of his mother, who looks at the two in happy amazement. Johanna is very tired from walking around the city. Her broken ribs are really hurting now, and she seems overcome with sadness. Esther tries to comfort her. From the ship, they view the lights of Gotenhafen in the fading daylight. The last rays of the sunset cast long shadows from the ship onto the harbor waters.

"Esther, I always enjoyed hearing your violin playing in the evenings in Ludwigsburg. There is so much heart and soul in it. Would you play something for us now? Please, Esther?" Johanna's eyes plead with Esther.

"What about the sonata, the one you wrote in Lübeck?" Peter adds. "It has such power to stir the emotions." The others likewise urge Esther.

"Joachim, would you please go and bring the violin to me?" Esther asks. When the violin arrives, she unpacks it with tender care. She looks at it for a while, as if lost in thought. "I will play you the second movement from my sonata," Esther announces.

Now, quite a few of the passengers come and sit around Esther. After carefully tuning the violin, she tugs the violin under her chin with resoluteness. Her bow hovers over the string in anticipation, as if waiting for a conductor's baton to release the silent agony. Then a powerful stroke of the bow that seems incongruous with her delicate arm creates a sonorous, low A that vibrates the air, sending shivers down the listeners' spine. The bow suddenly rips across the strings to an A two octaves higher, where it wails for a second or two, with a strong vibrato, before a flurry of descending arpeggios brings it back to the low A. Then a pause, before a slow, plaintive, unmistakably Jewish melody fills the air. It awakens feelings of loss and sadness, hope and despair. More people come rushing over to share the moment. A sudden departure from the slow melody brings on a rush of notes that are loaded with passion, aggression, even anger—sounds that want to squeeze life out of the listener but struggle for survival, then gradually give up the struggle in total acquiescence, submitting themselves to the dominance of the opening melody.

When she finishes playing, the spellbound audience breaks into applause. There are few dry eyes in sight. With a polite "thank you," Esther packs her violin away and hands it to Joachim to take it back to its place. The passengers disperse quietly in the rapidly descending darkness. Johanna is overwhelmed and has dissolved in tears. When she composes herself, she says, "It brings back so many memories, so many thoughts that I kept hidden inside me, and you released them all with the strokes of your violin bow. Oh, Esther, you have such a wonderful gift to communicate the unspeakable." She leans over and kisses Esther gently on her forehead.

"Thank you, Johanna. We all carry the scars of our lives in our hearts. Music reveals and often heals them all. Good night, my friend." Esther returns the kiss.

They all rise to settle down for the night. Joachim and Elisabeth are ahead, chatting as they walk along. Esther hears something about marzipan.

When the first rays of the sun signal the start of the next day, the ship casts off and begins its journey to Riga, its next port of call. The gentle, lapping waves of the calm sea on the ship's bow wake the last of the sleeping passengers. A few fishing boats, basking in morning sunlight and pulling in the haul in their nets, are a spectacular sight.

In good weather and a steady southerly wind, they reach Riga, Latvia, in six days. The ship restocks for the long leg to St. Petersburg with a short stop at Tallinn in Estonia. The weather starts to change to a north-westerly wind as the ship sails along the coast of Estonia, but it is somewhat sheltered by the islands in the Gulf of Riga. However as the ship passes these islands and heads into the Gulf of Finland, the full force of the wind stirs up the sea and the passengers are once again subject to seasickness from the large waves rolling the ship from side to side. Below decks are people on their knees praying aloud to Mary to save them, whereas up on deck the Russian crew curses God as they battle the elements. People try to comfort one another. The crew has no time to give attention to them, as they try to save the ship from being driven onto the rocky shoreline. The sun is not visible, as massive dark clouds cover land and sea. The ship wallows in the heavy seas and now truly resembles the picture of an elephant, as the name of the ship, *Slon*, suggests. Its creaking boards give some passengers foreboding thoughts that the ship may break up. Every time there is a particularly loud creak of the wooden boards some passengers let out a soulful cry as if death is imminent. Joachim, who is handling the rough seas better now, sits with Elisabeth and her parents.

Just when hope is at its lowest point, they all go quiet and listen. "The howling winds are abating," someone shouts from one end. "We are going to be all right!" Then, as fickle as the spring weather is, a capricious wind change from the south gradually calms the sea. The captain issues some vodka to his crew, who warm their cold and wet bodies and cheer up their spirits.

The next morning, Tallinn comes into view and everyone feels a lot more cheerful. The inns near the pier provide the most delicious Estonian cuisine; pork and potatoes in heavy gravy with sauerkraut is most passengers' choice. Esther and Joachim and the Stork family do not eat pork, for religious reasons, so they opt for some Estonian black bread and chicken-vegetable soup. Johanna decides not to eat the pork out of respect for her friends, so she too eats the bread and soup.

As he serves their food, their waiter says, "*Jätku leiba*," meaning "May your bread last," the Estonian equivalent of the German expression "*guten Appetit*" or the French "*bon appétit*." Joachim looks across the table at Elisabeth, whose pale complexion is gradually gaining some color. Once they all have eaten and felt the dry land under their feet for a day, a happy, positive mood returns and they begin looking forward to arriving in St. Petersburg. From Tallinn, it is a perfect four-day journey under the most favorable of conditions.

Chapter 7
Entry into the Promised Land

*"Prosperity is not without many fears and distastes;
and adversity is not without comforts and hopes." —Francis Bacon*

THE HARBOR TOWN OF KRONSTADT IS THE PORT OF DISEMBARKATION. SOME PASSENGERS REMARK ON THE NAME KRONSTADT'S HARDLY SOUNDING LIKE A RUSSIAN NAME. And they are right—it is not a Russian but a Swedish name, a painful reminder to the Russians of the war with Sweden and the Swedish occupation of this region. It was the Swedes who founded and named the city. When it comes into full view, passengers eagerly go to the port side of the ship to get a glimpse of the "promised land." All hardships of the journey are forgotten, replaced by their cherished hopes to make their fortunes in Russia. They all chat away animatedly. Esther, who is somewhat older than Peter, holds his arm on one side, while Johanna, a good ten years younger, holds Peter's other arm. Joachim stands next to his mother. "Peter, how sure are you that we as Jews are going to be accepted here in Russia?" he says, leaning across to address Peter.

"I cannot be certain, Joachim, but you are not entering as poor Jews—you have capital, and your mother has skills that are desirable to the Russian state. There is good reason to be confident, yes?"

The Stork family, standing nearby, has overheard Joachim's question. "Oh, Papa, what if they don't let Joachim in? I could not bear it," Elisabeth pleads with her father.

"I have a letter of commission from the Tsarina herself. If needed, I can persuade the authorities to let them through as part of my group of assistants: Peter as the architect, Johanna as the jeweller..."

"They are not the problem; they are not Jews, Papa!"

"Do not worry about us, Aaron," says Esther. "I will deal with that when it comes to it. I have learned much about dealing with Russian authorities from the Mendelssohn financiers in Stuttgart. They knew how to 'speak their language,' if you know what I mean."

The group is astounded by Esther's ingenuity, resoluteness, and confidence. "Are you sure you can 'talk' with them?" asks Peter.

"I already have all my papers in order; they are lined with five hundred gulden. That is roughly fifteen hundred rubles. They 'speak that language' very well."

"I hope and pray that it will work," Elisabeth says as she comes over to unashamedly grab Joachim's arm.

Disembarking is delayed until the next morning, April 3, 1756, as the titular counselor, Ivan Kuhlberg, with his rather German-sounding surname, did not arrive on April 2. Punctuality is not a particular trademark of Ivan Kuhlberg. When he finally arrives, the smell of vodka is all over him like the dense fog that still lies over the harbor. He brings with him the papers to make a list for the Chancery of Oversight of Foreigners. This list is a comprehensive document that details the ship's port of departure, travel dates, name, owners, captain's name, et cetera. All passengers are listed individually by name and family and religion, along with their place of birth or origin, as well as their occupation.

It becomes obvious quite quickly that the clerks and supervisors do not have a good grasp of German. For anyone Jewish, the clerks dislike for them, presents another problem. Prior to the rule of Tsar Peter the Great, Jews were forbidden to enter Russia. However, during his reign, Tsar Peter the Great recruited many foreign artists and highly skilled men of various professions to his new capital, St. Petersburg, to make it a grand place for art and learning. Many highly skilled Jews found a new home in the city as administrators, as well as serving in the court of the Tsar, after converting to become Eastern Orthodox Christians. The Tsarina Elizabeth still holds to the practice, but not with the same enthusiasm as Peter the Great. The mood is changing, and the Jewish population is taking precautions by keeping as low a profile as is practical. While the nobility still seek the advantage of having Jewish businesspeople and artisans in their employ, the grassroots citizens are becoming envious of their success and their accolades.

The clerk questions the Stork family carefully when he notes that they are Jews. However, when Aaron produces the letter of commission from the Tsarina Elizabeth, they quickly process his papers. Aaron also speaks for Peter and Johanna as members of his team of workers. The clerk carefully examines their trade skills and then lets them through with their visas and work permits. Esther and Joachim are among the last to be processed. The Stork family, Johanna, and Peter are waiting for them outside the barriers. Elisabeth looks anxiously back to where Esther and Joachim are. Esther is called up to fill in the details on their list. However, she does not hand over all of her documents, only the relevant items for immigration purposes. The clerk notes *Jewish* under "Religion." He stops and looks searchingly at Esther. When she finally presents her completed immigration papers, the Russian clerk says in his hacked, gruff German, "*Wo ist Mann?* [Where is your husband?]"

"*Er ist tot* [he is dead]," Esther replies.

"*Nein, er dein Mann,*" he says, pointing to Joachim as if he were Esther's husband.

"*Nein, er ist mein Junge.* [No, he is my son.]" Esther becomes firm in her speech.

"*Lüge nicht! Er ist grosser Mann!* [Don't lie! He is a big man!]" shouts the clerk.

Esther can see their point, for Joachim has the large frame of his father, and big hands. Yet suddenly it dawns on Esther what they are doing. If Joachim is her "husband," he has no trade or skill and cannot enter into Russia under her name. Esther resists the urge to speak with the clerk in Russian but continues in German: "I want to see your boss. I am not moving or doing anything until I speak with the boss—you understand?" Esther demands.

"*Verstehe, verstehe* [understand, understand]," says the clerk, and throwing up his hands he goes off to call Ivan Kuhlberg, who takes Esther and Joachim into a separate room by himself. Kuhlberg pompously seats himself behind his desk, facing Esther. His vodka breath almost chokes her. He lights his cigar, takes a satisfying lungful of smoke, blows it into the air, and slumps back in his comfortable chair. He looks her over with his sleazy, lecherous eyes and says in German, "*Schöne Frau!* [Beautiful woman!]"

What a signal! Esther thinks. She instantly recognizes that Kuhlberg is a man who can be bought with "favors" or maybe money. However, she ignores that comment and begins a new tack in French: "*Monsieur, parlez-vous français, le langage utilise à la cour impériale de la Tsarine Elizabeth?* [Sir, do you speak French, the language of the imperial court of Empress Elizabeth?]"

Kuhlberg is taken aback by the reference to the Tsarina and stutters, "*Oui, oui, bien sûr. Avez-vous un problème?* [Yes, yes, of course. Do you have a problem?]"

"*Oui, un probléme énorme.* Joachim"—she points at him - *c'est mon fils, et pas mon mari, vous comprenez? Il a quatorze ans.* [Yes, a big problem. Joachim here, he is my son, not my husband, understand? He is fourteen years old.]"

"*Pardonnez-moi, madame, pouvez-vous me presenter vos papiers, s'il vous plaît?* [Excuse me, madam, can you please give me your papers?]"

Esther now carefully hands him *all* the papers and watches Kuhlberg like a hawk. Kuhlberg opens the pages and sees the money. A momentary reaction in his eyes tells Esther, *Bingo!*

However, he pretends he does not see it and works his way through the papers for what seems an eternity. He leans back in his chair, in a contemplative mood, and takes another satisfying puff on his cigar, blowing the smoke into the air. In Russian, he mutters something like, "What a waste of a beautiful woman who has no husband to sleep with." Esther ignores him, but Joachim, who understands every word, twitches his right arm. Esther grabs it without Kuhlberg's seeing it. She does not want Kuhlberg to know that they speak Russian, and certainly does not want Joachim to do something that will jeopardize their visas. All she knows is that she has played her ace card and her fate lies here, with this creature called Kuhlberg.

Finally, he closes the papers and stuffs them into his heavy coat pocket. He then writes out her visa papers and work permit. He hands them to Esther, looks up into her eyes, and says, in French: "Everything is in perfect order, madam. I will advise the clerk to let you through." As he opens the door to let Esther and Joachim out, he says with a broad smile, "Your 'German' papers were *very* well documented." Then in Russian: "*Do svidaniya* [good-bye]." Then he adds cynically, "You will get along better learning Russian than your 'imperial' French." He then shouts over to the clerk to let Esther go through.

Esther breathes silently with relief, and with a very slight nod of her head and a curtsy, she says in Russian, "Thank you so much for all your troubles. I am very grateful to you." Kuhlberg raises his eyebrows and whistles quietly, wondering what else she understood. When she is a little farther along, she stops. "What did Kuhlberg mean by 'your *German* papers'?" She quickly opens her documents, and to her shock and surprise and even a little annoyance, she notes that he entered her as a "German" citizen. There is no reference to her being a Jewess. Kuhlberg has also, with a stroke of the pen, converted her religion to Russian Orthodox. For a moment she wants to turn and have it out with Kuhlberg, but then she reasons that this may come to be useful in the future.

"I am a Jewess. No piece of paper can change that. Maybe Kuhlberg was so impressed with my 'documents' that he wanted to do me a great favor. Well, so be it. I won't tell anybody—and neither will you, Joachim," she says, leaning over to his ear.

The smile on Joachim's face signals to the rest of the waiting group that all is well and that they can finally breathe a sigh of relief. Meanwhile, Peter takes firm control of the locked case containing Esther's money, as she asked him to. They all load their luggage into a waiting coach and make their way into the magic city of St. Petersburg, where they find a pleasing guesthouse to stay in for a few days while they make their final plans. That evening they have a fabulous feast and a bottle of French champagne to celebrate their arrival in the "promised land." They wish each other all the best and hope that God will bless their new start in life with wealth and happiness.

Chapter 8
St. Petersburg, 1756

"If a man will begin with certainties, he shall end in doubts; but if he will be content to begin with doubts, he will end in certainties."
—Francis Bacon

THE OPULENCE THAT PETER THE GREAT CREATED IS QUICKLY RECOGNIZABLE IN THE ELABORATE ARCHITECTURE OF THE CITY. They see Trinity Square, where Peter the Great had his cabin before building his palace. They pass the market where visiting merchants display their goods amid the bustling population of 150,000. Near the banks of the river Neva are some nice inns and bars. It is obvious that the monarch has given much attention to the city's appearance, especially since he moved the seat of government from Moscow to St. Petersburg. Most impressive is the city of Petrodvorets and its Grand Palace, a residence with lavish gardens and fountains that rivals Versailles in France. Equally impressive are the Winter Palace and the Smolny Cathedral, the creations of the baroque architect Bartolomeo Rastrelli. The city is so opulent that it challenges most of the great cities of Europe. Peter Hardt is like a walking encyclopedia as he points out the specific features of baroque architecture, a style he is thoroughly familiar with from his education in Heidelberg, Germany. He is particularly impressed by the buildings called the Twelve Colleges. That architectural style is typical of the Italian baroque movement. His eye is so finely tuned that he is able to discern the differences between the German- and the Italian-style baroque buildings. He is also able to note the influences of a new style of architecture, which creates buildings with clean, uncluttered lines, omitting all ornate features.

On a few buildings, Peter stops to point out something interesting. He refers to the catastrophic fire that ravaged the city fewer than twenty years ago, during the reign of Tsarina Anna. "Although restoration is generally meticulous, here and there you see very clearly (Peter points to the roof of a building) a feature that embodied the changing style." Esther is enthralled with Peter's knowledge on this subject. "The word 'baroque' is an interesting description of art, architecture, and music," Peter continues. "It has only recently come into vogue to describe the ornate style and to distinguish it from the new style of building and, dare I say, even the arts. It seems almost unbelievable that baroque' actually means 'grotesque.' However, it must be remembered that such a name is given to this style by those promoting the new style in order to make the old seem unattractive, even obsolete."

"Nevertheless, good craftsmen and artisans must be thoroughly familiar with all the styles, especially when working to restore or amend certain buildings and works of art, as with, for example, the work we will have to do on the Amber Room," Aaron adds.

"I wonder," says Esther, "if the style of music so powerfully defined by Bach and Handel and Telemann will also give way to the new era. I cannot wait to get back into the music business. I feel so alive and excited about living and working in this wonderful city that is so imbued with a love of the arts."

By April 9, everyone's plans seem to be formulated. Over a pleasurable dinner at a restaurant near the river Neva, they all reveal what they have accomplished and what they hope to accomplish yet. Peter announces that he has found a Czech coachbuilder, by the name of Vladimir Zázvorková, who wants to see Joachim, with an eye toward apprenticing him for the next five years. Joachim is pleased at this prospect, but very subdued.

St. Petersburg, 1756

"*Vladimir? Vladimir?*" Esther scratches around in the recesses of her mind, as if that name should mean something, but now she dismisses it and relates how she has made contact with the fabulous St. Petersburg orchestra. She auditioned on Monday in front of the conductor, the concertmaster, and a select number of orchestra principals. Her visa, work permit papers, and CV were checked and accepted. She will soon start rehearsals. "This is probably no regular income, but maybe the payments for performances are very good. I was not told the conditions of my work with the orchestra. I will probably seek some employment in the finance business for regular income," Esther speaks enthusiastically.

"How did you manage, as a Jewess, to be accepted into the orchestra without the express approval of the Tsarina?" Ruth questions. "We had to have a letter from her to get a work permit."

Esther was hoping that no one would ask this question but she cannot circumvent it and so reveals the incident at Kronstadt: "When Kuhlberg filled out my entry visa, he entered my citizenship simply as German. He forgot or deliberately did not state that I am Jewish. Perhaps because of my 'very good documentation,' as he put it. I beg you; please keep this secret between us."

As expected, Aaron and Ruth have made their arrangements to move to Zarskoje Selo, to begin his work on the Amber Room modification. Zarskoje Selo is not that far from St. Petersburg, but the imminent departure of the Stork family with Johanna seems hard to contemplate. A strong bond has formed between the Group of Seven. Elisabeth's eyes are filling with tears. Not only will she miss Joachim terribly, but she has become genuinely fond of Esther.

"And you, Peter, what will you do?" asks Ruth.

"Well, I have kept my promise to Uncle Alexander, and that is to find a coachbuilder for Joachim and to deliver Esther and Joachim safely to Russia.

Esther can hardly believe what Peter is saying. She feels like a piece of mail that the postman has just dropped into the letterbox.

Peter goes on: "So now I am free to go wherever there is architectural work for me."

Free? Esther now screams silently in her head. *What does he mean by "free"?* She wants to get up and run.

Peter grabs her by the arm. "Where are you going?"

"I need to go outside. I can't breathe."

Peter feels her trembling arm. "Esther, what is the matter?" Peter looks searchingly into Esther's eyes, which are filling with tears. Her face reveals devastation.

"I thought we…I mean you…I mean, I was hoping that…"

"Hoping that what, Esther?" Peter speaks emphatically and in a tone of voice she has never heard before, and that shocks her even more.

After a moment, Esther gathers her composure and says, "As I said to you in the coach while we were on the way to Lübeck, I should not, and will not now, take advantage of your friendship. You have done more for me than any person could ever ask for. For this and for your efforts to find Joachim a place where he can learn, I thank you deeply. Yes, you are 'free,' Peter—free to do what you must do." Inside, Esther is devastated. She has become very fond of Peter, and while there is no romance between them at present, there certainly are some sparks that may ignite love in the future. This she was hoping but dared not to express. *Perhaps it is the price one pays for observing social rules and not committing social taboos*, Esther ponders.

Johanna sits with her head bowed. The rest of the group sits in silent embarrassment at the sudden change in the dynamic. "I suppose you will go with Aaron to Zarskoje Selo?" Esther asks without looking at Peter.

"Esther, this is my big chance to get started in this country, to make something of myself, to earn money. I'm not like you. You are set up with money. I am just a poor architect." Peter's voice is becoming more and more aggressive. Esther is deeply shocked and hurt by the reference to her money. Johanna's head suddenly

St. Petersburg, 1756

swings up. She stares at Esther with her mouth wide open but says nothing. The party is over. Everyone heads back to their accommodations without saying good night. Elisabeth looks tearfully at Joachim. No one will sleep easy tonight.

✦

As the coach for Zarskoje Selo departs in the morning, Esther and Joachim stand alone, waving good-bye. Joachim is devastated. His youthful heart is breaking. They walk back into the guesthouse silently. Once inside, they fall into each other's arms and cry. "My heart is so sore, Mama. It feels the same as the day when Papa died," Joachim manages to say between sobs. Joachim has never mentioned his father in all these years. Esther feels Joachim's pain and her own disappointment. Now she is also reminded of Itzhak. "Mama, can you tell me about Papa? What was he like? I remember so little of him and even that is fading."

It is all too much for Esther to bear, and she falls on her bed and cries until there are no more tears. Joachim, too, goes to his bed, kneels down, and prays for Elisabeth's safety and well-being. He also prays for his mother, that she will come through this pain to live and find happiness again. Then he, too, falls asleep on his bed.

There is a knock on the door. "Madam Hahn, you have a visitor!" a Russian voice calls out.

Esther scrambles to her feet and rubs her eyes to wake up. "One moment," she calls. She quickly dresses herself and opens the door. In front of her stands Sergey Ivanov, conductor of the orchestra, a man highly regarded in the musical circles of the city and the court. Esther stands there as if rooted to the earth.

"May I come in?" Ivanov asks.

"Oh, yes, yes, oh, excuse me, I am a little flustered. Please do come in and sit down." Esther straightens her clothes hastily.

"Oh, you speak Russian very well," Ivanov compliments Esther.

"Well, I have been in Russia for nine whole days—I should have learned something." They both laugh out loud. His benign look shows that he likes Esther's sense of humour. "May I offer you a cup of tea?"

"That would be lovely, madam." While Esther makes the tea, Ivanov says, "I read your immigration papers and credentials. They are very impressive."

After taking a sip or two, Ivanov continues, "I did not have time to speak with you when you auditioned, but since we are starting rehearsal tomorrow—that is, Saturday at nine a.m.—I thought I would come personally to meet you so we can talk a little. I do so like to know my orchestra well. It makes for better cooperation and understanding. Now for the official part of my visit: I am offering you the second chair of the violins as associate concertmaster. Our previous associate concertmaster Bjorn Olaffsen, a Swede, has returned to Stockholm to take up a position as concertmaster. He was never happy here, as Swedes are not well liked in St. Petersburg because of the wars we had with them over the possession of this city."

In trying to comprehend this incredible change of fortune, Esther is left speechless, with her mouth wide open.

"Are you not happy with that offer?" asks Ivanov.

"Of course I am very happy, but pardon me if I am a little overcome with surprise." Esther can barely breathe.

"Oh, I forgot to tell you that you are, of course, a tenured, salaried member."

Esther's head reels even more. After a brief, pregnant pause, she suddenly asks, "Did you say tomorrow is Saturday?" with a little fright coming over her.

"Yes, indeed, tomorrow is Saturday," says he.

"Oh, my!" She puts her hand over her mouth as the realization sets in. "Then I must have slept for almost two days and nights."

Ivanov chuckles. "Perhaps I am the prince that wakes Sleeping Beauty?"

St. Petersburg, 1756

Esther smiles. Suddenly she says with a little panic, "Please excuse me. I must quickly check my son, he must have slept also." As she turns, she sees Joachim fully dressed.

"It's all right, Mother. I have been up during the two days. I have written a letter to Elisabeth. Then I found the postal service and sent the letter to her. It made me feel much better."

"Oh, Mr. Ivanov, may I introduce to you my son, Joachim? Joachim, this is Mr. Ivanov."

"I am pleased to meet you, Joachim."

"How do you do, Mr. Ivanov?"

"Now, madam, the other reason I called was to help you establish yourself in this city. Only settled and contented musicians make the finest music. I care for all the members of my orchestra. Tomorrow is a big day of rehearsals. We are preparing for the summer concerts. Among the many performances will be concerts at the Summer Palace, at the request of the Tsarina, and possibly one in Zarskoje Selo." Esther blushes a little, and Joachim's heart leaps. "So, after rehearsals, would you and Joachim do me the honor of dining with me at my humble home?" Esther is surprised at the invitation but gladly accepts. "Fine, then I shall look forward to seeing you at the rehearsal. There will be a coach waiting for you at eight a.m. to take you to the music academy. Until then!" He takes Esther's hand and kisses it gently, bows, and leaves.

Esther still is half asleep and thinks she is dreaming, when Ivanov knocks again with the apology that he has forgotten to tell her that a woman from the orchestra administration, by the name of Olga, will call later to take her to have her performance clothes made by a seamstress, as well as to buy a dress for the dinner party. Esther attempts to object. "No, no, no," says Ivanov and waves his index finger, "this is all paid for and part of the orchestra's expenses." Esther is stunned. "And here is your portfolio with the music for the summer program; you may wish to have a quick look at it before tomorrow. *Do svidaniya,*" Ivanov leaves again.

"Joachim!" Esther shouts with unbridled joy. "Let's have breakfast. I am ab-so-lu-te-ly famished!"

Esther makes arrangements for Joachim to spend the day with Mr. Zázvorková, so that they can get acquainted with each other. Mr. Zázvorková greets Joachim, introduces himself, and asks what language Joachim prefers to speak with him. Joachim states that it is German, but that he can speak Russian quite well. Mr. Zázvorková shows Joachim his workshop and some of the coaches that are being built. "So, your name is Joachim Hahn? And you are a Jew, aren't you?" he inquires. "Where are you from?"

"I was born a Jew in Ludwigsburg," Joachim answers.

"And your father?"

"He was born in Stuttgart, but he died a few years ago in Frankfurt."

"This is just amazing," exclaims Zázvorková.

"Why is that so amazing, sir?" Joachim inquires. "Now, let me see—your father's name was Itzhak, am I correct? And your grandfather was Salomon. He was a coachbuilder in Stuttgart and then moved to Ludwigsburg by the invitation of the Duke."

Joachim is gob-smacked. "How do you know all this?"

"That is easy, my boy—I learned my trade from your grandfather in Stuttgart. Your father, Itzhak, was like a brother to me, and all these years I have wondered what happened to him. Now here you stand in front of me, the mirror image of your father, with his broad shoulders and his large, powerful hands. Let me show you something, Joachim." He takes Joachim into his workshop and opens a little drawer inside the cupboard where his precious tools are. "Your grandfather taught me to look after my tools," he says proudly. When he opens the drawer, Joachim sees a bronze cast about the size of his large palm. "What do you see, Joachim?"

"It is a likeness of a rooster *[Hahn]* encircled by a ring." Joachim looks at Vladimir as if something is dawning in his mind. "This is not…?"

St. Petersburg, 1756

"Yes, Joachim, this is the insignia that your grandfather designed for all his coaches, and I am sure your father, Itzhak, used it as well. Joachim, you are the rightful heir to this item. Please take it and take good care of it." Joachim is still stunned but accepts it graciously. "Now, will I take you on as my apprentice? Of course I will, of course!" shouts Vladimir, and hugs Joachim. Then he adds, "This is the best day of my life and the best way to thank your family for having taken me in as a lad and taught me this wonderful trade. Come, Joachim, meet my wife, Dasha, and let us celebrate."

✦

On Saturday morning, Esther takes her violin, her music, and her new dress, ready for the dinner at Sergey Ivanov's house later on. The coach arrives punctually at 8:00 a.m. Ivanov is there at the music academy to welcome her. Before rehearsals begin, she meets some of her colleagues, among them Mikhail Ordowsky, a tall, proud Russian violinist educated at the Italian schools. Esther feels right at home but is unaware that Ordowsky questions her ethnicity. He approaches Ivanov with his concerns, but Ivanov assures him that her papers state that she is German and of the Russian Orthodox religion. Ordowsky acquiesces but is not happy. "She looks like a Jewess. Even her name is Jewish. No one can convince me that she is not, papers or no papers," he mutters.

The 9:00 a.m. bell rings, and so begins the hard work. However, before the rehearsal commences, Esther is introduced as the new associate concertmaster, to the happy applause of the orchestra. Ordowsky gently taps his left hand with his violin bow, a gesture that does not go unnoticed by either Esther or Ivanov. Rehearsal goes till twelve noon, and then from 1:00 p.m. to 5:00 p.m., with a small break at three.

By the end of the first day, Esther is thoroughly exhausted. There is a lot of homework to do before the next rehearsal, but she feels alive inside and is thriving on the challenge of her newfound life. Ivanov goes over to her and congratulates her, as do the concertmaster and then a procession of her colleagues, all shaking her hand.

"I have ordered my coach to collect Joachim. You may change your clothes here, in the dressing rooms. Please wait for me here when you are dressed." Ivanov departs with a smile and a nod of his head.

When Esther is dressed, Ivanov comes to fetch her. He stops dead in his tracks when he sees her. Thirty-eight-year-old Esther looks absolutely, serenely stunning in her black-and-gold brocade evening dress. "Pardon my reaction, Madam Hahn, but you look unbelievably beautiful in this dress," Ivanov manages to say. Esther blushes a little at such a compliment. Ivanov slings a lovely cape over her ivory shoulders, since it is still cool at night, and then offers his arm to escort Esther to the coach, where Joachim is already waiting.

Once in the coach, Ivanov asks Joachim about his day with Mr. Zázvorková. Joachim overflows with excitement as he relates the story of Mr. Zázvorková and his father growing up together as apprentices to his grandfather Salomon. Then he reveals the bronze insignia Mr. Zázvorková gave him. Esther recognizes it immediately and then it dawned on her: "That's the Vladimir I heard your father speak of," she said.

"He was sad that Papa had died, as he would have loved to meet up with him again," Joachim finishes. In all, Joachim had the most wonderful day at the workshop. Ivanov is quietly pleased that the information about Esther's husband is revealed without his having to ask for it, as it may have seemed impolite.

"What about you, Mama?" Joachim asks. "How did your first day go at the orchestra?"

Before Esther can answer, Ivanov chimes in: "Oh, it was terrible, Joachim; your mother made so many mistakes, but"—he shrugs his shoulders and moves his head slightly to the side—"we decided to keep her anyway." Ivanov smiles and they all laugh. He is pleased that Esther likes his kind of humor.

"Then I presume you had a good day, Mama," Joachim states enthusiastically. "And it will get better. We have not had dinner yet, have we?" Ivanov raises his eyebrows. "Oh, I'm so hungry," says Joachim.

"Your manners, Joachim!" Esther chides him.

"It's all right. It was not so long ago that I should have forgotten what a hungry, growing boy feels like. Just be yourself, Joachim; I do not like my guests to stand on ceremony in my company," Ivanov says, putting this awkward moment into the proper perspective.

✧

"Welcome to my humble house," Ivanov bows slightly. His house is anything but humble. A servant opens the door of the coach and helps Esther out. The outside of the house is a magnificent example of the baroque style, which Peter has taught her to identify. The lobby is elaborately lit by a large crystal chandelier reflecting sparkles of light onto the gilded decor and paintings against a deep, regal red color. A servant girl approaches, curtsies, and takes Esther's cape and Joachim's overcoat. Ivanov then takes the two on a grand tour of his house.

"So, this is your humble home?" Esther gives Ivanov a cheeky smile.

"Well, I've made it a little more comfortable in recent years," he says with great modesty.

Admiring the paintings, Esther points to a particular portrait of a very fine woman. "May I ask who this lady is?"

"She is my wife...I mean, was—she died eight years ago in childbirth."

"I'm so sorry, Mr. Ivanov." Esther reaches out to take his hand out of sheer habit of compassion, but retracts it before touching him. She hopes he did not see this accidental indiscretion.

"I had difficulties getting over her tragic death." He continues, "You see, just when our expectation for happiness reached the pinnacle, she, and the child, were ripped away from me." He remains silent while looking at the picture.

"What was her name?" Esther asks to break the silence.

"Marie Antoinette," he says in a very subdued voice.

"I'm so sorry, Mr. Ivanov. I did not mean to bring up so much pain," Esther apologizes.

"Please don't apologize—I am learning to live again. May I confess to you that you and Joachim are my first guests in this house since Marie Antoinette died?"

Esther feels a sharp pain in her heart for Ivanov's loss as she is silently reminded of her own loss.

"Thank you for sharing your treasured memories of your wife. You are a very brave man Mr. Ivanov," Esther says with deep sincerity.

Just then, the dinner is announced, and they proceed to the dining table.

They find the meal absolutely delicious. Joachim politely thanks his host, to the obvious approval of his mother. While they are enjoying a glass of fine port, Ivanov says in a pensive manner, "You remember yesterday, when I called at the guesthouse, I said I want to help you get settled? So, I suppose you will need some permanent housing for yourself and Joachim; you cannot stay in that wretched guesthouse forever. You will need your privacy to practice the violin and to feel settled. May I be so free as to make a suggestion to you?" he asks.

Esther is flustered inside. *Surely he is not offering for me to live here—no, no, that is very presumptuous of me to think.* So she says, "All right, what do you suggest?"

St. Petersburg, 1756

"As you may know," he begins, "the military, that is swarming this city, and whose soldiers have been living in private homes all over the place, has begun to be taken to proper military establishments: one on Ligovsky Canal, another on Gorohovaya Street, and a third on Zagorodney Prospect. That leaves a lot of houses on the market for a good price. I looked at one just off Nevsky Prospect, one of the main streets running up from the Admiralty. It would suit you and Joachim perfectly, for it is also within walking distance of Mr. Zázvorková's workshop. The asking price is fifteen thousand rubles. Now, I can help—"

"Mr. Ivanov," Esther interrupts, "I have that kind of money. But if you would help me find a nice place, I will most graciously accept. But first of all, can you help me to bank my money and to exchange it for rubles?" "There is a Jew called Ginsburg making quite a name for himself as a banker. I think we should go and see what he has to offer," Ivanov suggests. He is anxious to help Esther and so he suggests that they might attend to these matters the next day.

Esther and Ivanov visit Ginsburg and are pleased with the business arrangements Ginsburg makes for Esther's money. Esther then withdraws from her account fifteen thousand roubles and safely tugs the money into the inside pocket of her coat.

Ivanov is eager to show her the houses that have become vacant. Esther is pleased with a number of them, but looks to Ivanov for approval. They finally decide on 30 Kazanskaya Ulitska, a splendid street with magnificent buildings. Ivanov takes Esther and Joachim on Sunday to have another look. On Monday, Ivanov accompanies Esther to sign the papers to buy the house. Esther feels that Ivanov is doing too much for her and suggests that she might do it on her own. "I will come with you. You will see why," Ivanov insists, and Esther acquiesces.

When they arrive, the clerk presents the papers and Esther tables her documents. The clerk looks at them, takes the papers, and disappears into another room, where his superior's office is.

After a little while, he emerges and says, "I'm sorry, madam, you are an unmarried woman; you cannot own a house in St. Petersburg."

"But," Esther objects, "there are many unmarried women in St. Petersburg who own property."

"Indeed, madam," he says, bowing gently, "but they are all women of nobility, with connections."

Esther is devastated. *More discrimination,* she thinks. *I wonder if he suspects that I am a Jewess. The "wolves" are everywhere."*

"May I speak with your superior, please, sir?" asks Ivanov.

"Certainly sir. Step this way." The clerk ushers Ivanov into the office. When Ivanov returns, the clerk's boss calls him back. A little while later, he comes out with a smile and says, "Mr Ivanov, you may sign for Madam Hahn, and nothing more will be said."

Esther hands over 15,000 rubles and receives the ownership papers and the key to the house.

"Do you now see why I came?" asks Ivanov. Esther nods her head, and then looks at Ivanov with grateful eyes glistening with moisture. "May I give you a congratulatory kiss, Madam Hahn?" Ivanov asks hopefully.

"Of course you may," she says warmly.

He kisses her cheeks, and then dries Esther's eyes with his handkerchief. The warmth of his lips sends a shiver down her spine. "Now, I am taking you to a nice restaurant for lunch and a glass of French champagne—I insist!" He lifts his finger to stop Esther's protest.

During lunch, Esther asks, "What did you say to the clerk's superior that made him change his mind?"

"Madam Hahn, there is a very persuasive language spoken here in St. Petersburg. It is called 'rubles.'"

Esther bursts out laughing.

"Why are you so amused by this?" Ivanov asks.

"Because I had to use that language on Ivan Kuhlberg to persuade him to let me enter into Russia…Oh, I'm sorry, I should not have mentioned that." Esther looks with terrified eyes at Ivanov.

St. Petersburg, 1756

"Why not, Esther? Why should you not tell me that? Do you not think me astute and caring enough to check you out thoroughly?" He reaches across the table to hold Esther's trembling hand. "Don't be afraid, Esther; your secret is safe with me. I will never use it against you or take advantage of you over this matter." Esther almost collapses with gratitude. "Now, do tell me what happened with Kuhlberg," Ivanov says. Esther then tells him the whole story, which amuses him greatly.

❖

Over the next five years, Joachim finishes his apprenticeship with Vladimir Zázvorková.

He and Vladimir visit Zarskoje Selo a few times on business. Joachim is always glad to catch up with Elisabeth and her parents. Esther, too, visits both privately and with the orchestra. Johanna is always busy and does not spend much time with Esther. Peter, on the other hand, does not let go an opportunity to speak with Esther. However, it is obvious to both of them that any spark of romance is well and truly extinguished. One of their last meetings in Zarskoje Selo is in the summer of 1759, when the orchestra performs the spectacular oratorio *The Messiah* in Zarskoje Selo in honor of the late Georg Friedrich Händel, who died on April 14 of this year.

Time passes quickly for Esther in this magical city. The summers are full of performances, balls at fashionable venues, dinner parties, and socializing in the Summer Garden. The winters are cold and demand determination to keep going, yet the snow that covers the city in the winter evenings under the streetlights has a romantic feel for her. Horse-drawn sleighs gliding along the streets with men and women rugged up in their fur coats, going to ballet performances, are a pretty sight. Sleigh rides with Ivanov into the surrounding forests are both exhilarating and somewhat fearful. Snow hangs from fir trees like the bearskin overcoats on Russian peasants. Often, wolves howl in the distance, sending shivers down

Esther's spine. However, Ivanov never takes any chances. He always has two armed guards with him.

During one of these romantic outings Ivanov says, "Madam Hahn, do you not think it a little too formal to address each other as 'madam' and 'mister' when we have known each other for some five years? I would prefer for you to call me Sergey."

"Very well, then, Sergey, you may call me Esther."

"Thank you, Esther." Sergey reaches around Esther's shoulders and pulls her toward him.

Esther responds and snuggles up to him. *Such a feeling of security!* she thinks. Then, spontaneously, she pulls Sergey's head closer to hers and kisses him passionately. Sergey is totally surprised, pleasantly so, and looks at Esther, who seems absolutely serene. Then they both burst into laughter and hug each other. Esther acknowledges that Sergey has always acted in the most honorable and gentlemanly manner and never takes advantage of her vulnerable situation.

"I am vulnerable too, Esther. We both are, but we respect each other. That is what is so beautiful about our relationship." Now he returns the kiss.

❂

Esther spends more and more time in Sergey's company. They plan the orchestra's concerts and visits to Moscow and to Helsinki, in Finland. With Sergey's help, Esther reworks her sonata into a full concerto for violin and orchestra, which is to premier in the summer of 1761. But difficulties with Mikhail Ordowsky started to make life precarious. All along, he has resented Esther's position as associate concertmaster, and he has made secret inquiries about her, as he suspects that she is a Jewess. He has also found out that Joachim is apprenticed to Vladimir Zázvorková. Ordowsky secretly paid someone to befriend one of the other apprentices

St. Petersburg, 1756

of Zázvorková and bribe him to find out if Joachim is a Jew. That would make Esther a Jewess, since Judaism is passed on through the mother.

Having secured that vital piece of information, Ordowsky now has his ace card in his possession, waiting to play it when it counts most. Now that the first chair is becoming vacant, due to Borodin's upcoming retirement, Ordowsky plans to make his move. He wants that chair, if not the conductorship. He secretly mentions it to some select members of the orchestra, and that he hopes to petition the now-ailing Tsarina whose health began to decline after a series of dizzy spells, to sack Ivanov for his blatant liaison with a Jewess, and for thereby neglecting the interests of all the members of the orchestra—indeed, the interests of the imperial court.

Ivanov, however, is an astute man. He saw long ago in Ordowsky's eyes that he was waiting for an opportune time to play his cards. He also has a great, loyal support base in the orchestra who inform him of Ordowky's intentions. Ivanov's credentials and reputation with the imperial court are impeccable. He quickly requests an audience with the Tsarina, which she grants. Ivanov explains the rebellion brewing in the orchestra and identifies Mikhail Ordowsky as the person plotting his downfall. He is open and honest about Esther. The Tsarina reminds Ivanov that Ordowsky may have a case. However, she is willing to hold off any attempts by Ordowsky until she hears from Ivanov about how he wishes to resolve the impasse. She trusts in Ivanov's wisdom. He thanks the Tsarina and wishes her a speedy recovery and good health.

On his way home, he stops at 30 Kazanskaya Ulitska. Esther is by herself and is almost ready to go to bed. Joachim is staying with Vladimir for the night. They have to leave very early to take a new coach to Zarskoje Selo. Esther opens the door with her silky dressing gown hugging her shapely form. "Please, come in, Sergey," she gestures. "Is everything all right?"

"My dear Esther, I am in a terrible predicament. I know whatever I am about to say may make me look like a foolish, even a selfish, man. I don't know where to start."

Esther walks up close to Sergey and kisses him tenderly. "How about we start with this?" she asks.

Sergey sits on the sofa, and Esther pours two vodkas. "Now relax, Sergey, and tell me the story from the beginning." When Sergey explains the difficulties at the orchestra, Esther says, "I knew what Ordowsky was up to from the beginning. Did you not see, Sergey, his reaction to my appointment as associate concertmaster?"

"Yes, I did, and I have also kept a close eye on him."

"So how are you going to resolve this 'impasse,' as the Tsarina put it?"

"This, my dear Esther, is the part that will make me look so selfish. Let me put it to you this way: if you were to marry a Russian national, one of the problems would be solved, but that would be the end of our close friendship, unless, of course..."

"Unless what, Sergey?"

Sergey wrings his hands, as if to squeeze out the next few words. "Unless...unless *I* was that Russian man." Then he hastily adds, waving his hands as if dismissing such a presumptuous idea saying: "But that would look so selfish, as if I wanted to marry you only to beat Ordowsky and to keep my job and yours" Now he speaks slowly and deliberately: "Whereas the real truth is that I am madly in love with you and have been ever since I met you. Oh, I'm such an idiot," Sergey chastises himself, with an emphatic slap on his forehead.

Esther looks at Sergey with that serene look that he saw in the sleigh the previous winter when she kissed him. She says, "Could you simplify the reason for your visit?"

Sergey drops to his knees and says, "Esther, my love, will you marry me?"

Esther can hardly hold back her tears of joy. She holds out her hand and lifts Sergey up. Now eye to eye with him, she says, "Yes, Sergey, I will marry you."

St. Petersburg, 1756

Sergey takes his fiancée in his arms and holds her close to him. Then he suddenly releases her and says, "Now, the next thing I have to say is going to make me look even more selfish. Esther, we cannot get married. Under Russian law, I cannot marry a Jewess. I know your entry visa does not state that, but before God and man, we and others know that you are a Jewess—a beautiful woman with a golden heart."

"Then I will convert to become an Orthodox Christian. After all, it is already on my paper. So, to be sure, I will make it official, because I cannot prove that I was baptized as Orthodox. Will that solve the 'impasse'?" Esther says this so nonchalantly that it takes Sergey by surprise.

"Yes, but, Esther—"

"No, Sergey, don't you think I have been thinking about this eventuality? I do not see it as a betrayal of my Jewish blood. I cannot change that I am a Jewess on the inside and always will be. I am changing my religion, not my blood. I have had enough of being hounded and degraded as a Jewess. There are predators everywhere I go. When I marry you as an Orthodox Christian, I will, at least on paper, be one of them. Is that solution acceptable to you, Sergey?"

Sergey can hardly wait to inform the Tsarina of his solution, which pleases her well. After all, many Jews have, in the past, converted to the Russian Orthodox faith in order to serve at the imperial court. She asks Ivanov to inform Ordowsky that she wishes to see him shortly. Now Esther begins her process of conversion and is duly baptized. Then Sergey prepares for the marriage, but not in St. Petersburg. He wants to keep the whole thing as quiet as he can. So they wed in Moscow on August 6, 1760. Joachim gives his mother away at the ceremony, and Vladimir is Sergey's best man. Elisabeth feels highly honored to be Esther's bridesmaid; both of them look radiant. Among the guests is the Stork family and Sergey's family. Peter also comes, but not Johanna.

At the reception, Esther unwraps a little parcel. Everyone is looking with anticipation what it contains. It is a violin made from marzipan. Esther relates the story of this violin to all present; she says: "Joachim handed me this violin in Lübeck and said, 'Come, Mama, eat your violin.' And I said, 'Oh, I could not destroy something so precious just to satisfy my desire for something I had never tasted before.' And then, turning to Peter, she says "What did you say to me in reply to my comment, Peter?"

Coughing and a little embarrassed, Peter recalls their conversation in Lübeck. Quoting it verbatim he says, "You are correct, Esther. 'Never destroy anything that is precious to you just to satisfy a craving for something new. But when you are ready for it, you will eat it, won't you?'"

Esther admits she was a little surprised by what she had then said to Peter: 'Yes, of course I will eat it—someday I will.' My friends, my son, and my dear husband, Sergey, today is that day." With that, the violin is cut up and everyone has a piece.

Joachim, who is sitting with Elisabeth at the reception, takes a piece of the marzipan and puts it into Elisabeth's mouth. She lets out a muffled groan of joy. "Now you have tasted the greatest manna from heaven—Lübeck marzipan," he says with a measure of great satisfaction. When she finishes relishing the glorious taste, she leans over and kisses Joachim, who is slightly embarrassed but loves it nevertheless. He looks at Elisabeth with admiration. She has grown into a beautiful young woman. Romance seems to be in the air for them.

✦

On their honeymoon, Sergey and Esther spend a little time getting to know the city of Moscow. It does not have the splendor

St. Petersburg, 1756

of St. Petersburg but is rapidly progressing as a centre of learning. They visit the first University of Moscow, founded only seven years earlier, in 1755, when Esther read about it in the newspaper in Rothschild's office in the Judengasse.

Back in St. Petersburg, Esther moves into Sergey's nice home. They will keep the house at 30 Kazanskaya Ulitska for as long as Joachim needs it. The following week is the famous last performance of the summer season, appropriately held in the Summer Garden, which is always a spectacular prom concert. The ailing Tsarina Elizabeth is also present. No one in the orchestra except the outgoing concertmaster, Borodin, is aware of the conductor's changed marital status.

The night of the concert, the concertmaster's customary entrance does not take place, to questioning looks from the orchestra members. Borodin is already seated, in Esther's usual chair. The oboist sounds his standard A and the violins begin to tune up, as does the rest of the orchestra.

Now Sergey enters, mounts the podium, and bows to the Tsarina and the audience, and then to the orchestra, which applauds him in their unique manner of stamping their feet. Next, he turns back to face the audience and says: "Your Imperial Majesty, nobles of the Russian court, ladies and gentlemen, welcome to this year's final performance of the summer concerts. We hope you will enjoy the program. However, before we begin, I have a very special announcement to make. As you have no doubt noted, the first chair, that of the concertmaster, is vacant. Mr. Borodin is taking a well-earned rest, and we wish him well in his retirement." Mr. Borodin stands up to a round of applause and sits down again. Members of the orchestra begin to nervously wonder where Esther is and who the new concertmaster might be. Ordowsky is panicking that it may be Esther.

"Now," Sergey continues, "we are pleased to announce Mr. Borodin's replacement—Esther Ivanova!"

Esther walks out, curtsies to the Tsarina, shakes Ivanov's hand and takes the first chair, to thunderous applause. Ivanov faces the Tsarina, who smiles and nods her head benignly. The orchestra is speechless. There is an awkward pause before they stamp their feet. Ordowsky is frozen. He can hardly believe his eyes and ears. He tries to whisper something through his clenched teeth to the violinist to his left, but in his rage, what he says is much louder than he expected: "He married the Jewish bitch!"

Sergey hears it and glares at him. Ordowsky's face turns bright red, for he is caught out well and truly. Sergey is about to lift his baton, the orchestra is ready to play, but rather he turns again to the audience, apologizes for this change in routine, and says, "Your Imperial Majesty, nobles of the Russian court, ladies and gentlemen, I somehow forgot to mention to you something very important. It would be very remiss of me not to mention that another, most honorable member of the orchestra will be leaving. Would you please give a round of applause to Mr. Ordowsky"—Sergey points to him and gestures for him to stand—"who has served this orchestra loyally over many years? Tonight will be his last performance. We shall miss him terribly."

All eyes are on the Tsarina to see her response. Since she only responds with a very brief and polite clap, the rest of the audience also respond with a measured, respectful applause and Ordowsky bows graciously, though reluctantly, to acknowledge it. His Russian blood is boiling, and he would challenge Ivanov there and then for such public humiliation, but on account of the Tsarina's presence, he refrains. The orchestra is stunned. No stamping of the feet this time. Ordowky's humiliation is almost complete. Now he hopes that the earth will open to swallow him up.

Sergey then turns, holds the baton suspensefully, looks at Ordowsky, and whispers sarcastically, "Play well, Mikhail, for tomorrow you will meet the Tsarina personally."

St. Petersburg, 1756

At this final humiliation, Ordowsky almost drops his bow. Then, with a powerful downbeat that releases all his frustration and anger, Sergey sets the concert aflame.

※

The police and the coroner arrive at Ordowsky's house at 10:00 a.m. the next day. After a little while, they carry a body out to a waiting hearse. Ordowsky never gets to meet the Tsarina. Instead, he "prepared to meet his maker." The coroner rules his death a suicide, but the newspaper *Sankt-Peterburgskie Vedomosti* publishes an obituary that praises this talented musician and the great loss his death represents to St. Petersburg's musical life. Esther is shocked and feels partially responsible. Sergey, however, puts the case into proper, logical perspective, as he always does. "The humiliation he suffered was nothing in comparison with what he had planned for you and me. If he had succeeded in persuading the Tsarina, you and I would have been made into a public spectacle. For the Jews in St. Petersburg, it would have meant hell! This is really ironic."

"Sergey, what is ironic about this?"

"There is a book in the Bible called by the same name as yours: Esther."

Was she not the queen of the Persian emperor?"

"Yes, she and the rest of the Jews were about to be killed because Haman had plotted with the king to destroy the Jews."

Esther asks, "And then what happened?"

"Risking her life, she pointed out to the king what Haman had plotted. The king then publicly humiliated Haman and hanged him on the gallows he had built for Esther's uncle Mordecai, and the Jews were able to defend themselves. That was then celebrated as *Yom Kippur* and still is, down to this very day." Sergey now asks, "Was God unhappy about that?"

"No, I don't think so."

"Do you not see, my dear Esther, what we did was just what your Biblical counterpart Esther did. We defended ourselves and saved our lives."

Esther looks at Sergey with wide-open eyes. "Oh, Sergey, you are so wise and righteous. I love you for that and a thousand other reasons."

※

January 5, 1762, begins a period of great changes and, for a while, uncertainty. Early on this calm, snow-covered day, the church bells of Saints Peter and Paul Cathedral began to ring in slow, muffled, sombre tones. People jump out of their beds and run to their windows to see what the meaning of this bell ringing might be. Yet everyone knows deep down that a death has occurred at the imperial court. News quickly spreads that the Tsarina Elizabeth has died. The impact on the city is unbelievable. All businesses stay closed. People in the streets cry unashamedly and comfort one another. The outpouring of grief is seen everywhere. The imperial court goes into swift action to arrange for the extravagant funeral of its much-loved empress.

Four days later, Peter III becomes the new Tsar of Russia. The Tsarina Elizabeth arranged, way back in 1742, for Pyotr III Fyodrovich, as he was then known, to come from Kiel in Germany, where he was born a prince to Peter the Great's sister, to come to Russia as the heir presumptive. Also well before his accession to the throne, Elizabeth arranged for him to marry his second cousin Sophia Augusta Frederica on August 21, 1745. The princess then took the name Ekaterina Alexeievna (Catherine Alexis). The marriage was unhappy from the start and marked by much infidelity on both sides.

After Peter III's accession to the throne, Russians are divided in their loyalty to him. Some detest him for being an "idiotic, drunken womanizer," as Catherine describes him. Others decry him for being very pro-Prussian and handing too much power to

St. Petersburg, 1756

the German emperor Frederick II. Still others love him for the many social and political reforms he instigates, resembling those of Peter the Great. His reign is short-lived. His wife, Catherine II, conspires against him and has him imprisoned; he is later murdered, on July 17 of 1762. Catherine quickly succeeds him on the Russian throne, whereupon she becomes known as Catherine the Great.

Although Catherine the Great is hungry for power, she does ingratiate herself to the Russians through her many enlightened reforms. The castle at Zarskoje Selo is now almost finished, and the Amber Room is completed, in all its glory. For those who worked on the project, this means that their visas expire, unless they find another commissioned work. Peter Hardt has built up quite a reputation with the Russian nobility as an architect, but with the main work done, he is wondering about his future. Peter actually detests the artificial life of the nobility. He does not see himself as part of their scene. He yearns for some peace and quiet in a rural setting where he can work with his hands. He still dreams of setting up a forge to work as a blacksmith, to put his powerful arms to use. A great wanderlust still lurks in his heart.

Aaron Stork's work is also almost completed, and he does not see a life for him in Russia. He and his family plan to return to Magdeburg. He has received an invitation to join in a venture to set up a fine-jewellery business there with another Jew.

Elisabeth Stork does not want to leave here, where her heart is. She would be devastated if her father took her away from Joachim. Aaron, although a kindly man, argues with her. "You cannot remain here by yourself as an unmarried woman. It is impossible, you understand—impossible!" he restates.

"Please, Papa, give me a month to think about it; please don't rush me into making any decisions," Elisabeth pleads.

Aaron reluctantly agrees. "But only one month, Elisabeth, only one month!" Aaron's index finger visibly reinforces the one-month time frame. "We also have a deadline to leave here," Aaron reminds his daughter.

Via a courier, she sends a letter to Joachim asking him to please come immediately to see her, as a crisis is looming. Two days later, Joachim arrives. Elisabeth falls into his arms and sobs. "Father wants to take me back to Germany, Joachim. My heart would simply break if I lost you."

"No Elisabeth, no! This is not going to happen," Joachim states with great determination. "I have a trade; I can work and support a wife. We are both over twenty years old. Can we not make our own decisions? Let me speak with your father."

Joachim emerges from the Storks' house. Elisabeth's parents follow him out. He walks up to Elisabeth, bends down on one knee, and says, "Elisabeth, will you marry me?"

"What? Are you serious?" she cries.

"Will you marry me, please?" Joachim repeats.

"Of course I will marry you, Joachim. I will, I will, I will." She jumps up and down like a little girl. Her happiness is unbounded.

One month later, a Jewish rabbi performs the marriage ceremony at Neu-Saratowka, which is near St. Petersburg. Elisabeth's parents, Esther and Sergey, and Peter and Johanna are there. Then they register their marriage in St. Petersburg in the registry for births, deaths, and marriages. Joachim then takes his wife to his house at 30 Kazanskaya Ulitska, where they begin to build their lives on hope and industriousness. The Storks depart for Germany a few days later.

※

July 22, 1763, is a most auspicious day. The newspaper *Sankt-Peterburgskie Vedomosti* and all major newspapers in Europe publish this article:

St. Petersburg, 1756

The Manifesto of the Empress Catherine II

Issued

July 22, 1763

By the Grace of God!

We, Catherine the second, by the Grace of God, Empress and Autocrat of all the Russians at Moscow, Kiev, Vladimir, Novgorod, Tsarina of Kasan, Tsarina of Astrachan, Tsarina of Siberia, Lady of Pleskow and Grand Duchess of Smolensko, Duchess of Esthonia and Livland, Carelial, Twer, Yugoria, Permia, Viatka and Bulgaria and others; Lady and Grand Duchess of Novgorod in the Netherland of Chernigov, Resan, Rostov, Yaroslav, Beloosrial, Udoria, Obdoria, Condinia, and Ruler of the entire North region and Lady of the Yurish, of the Cartalinian and Grusinian tsars and the Cabardinian land, of the Cherkessian and Gorsian princes and the lady of the manor and sovereign of many others. As We are sufficiently aware of the vast extent of the lands within Our Empire, We perceive, among other things, that a considerable number of regions are still uncultivated which could easily and advantageously be made available for productive use of population and settlement. Most of the lands hold hidden in their depth an inexhaustible wealth of all kinds of precious ores and metals, and because they are well provided with forests, rivers and lakes, and located close to the sea for purpose of trade, they are also most convenient for the development and growth of many kinds of manufacturing, plants, and various installations. This induced Us to issue the manifesto which was published last Dec. 4, 1762, for the benefit of all Our loyal subjects. However, inasmuch as We made only a summary announcement of Our pleasure to the foreigners who would like to settle in Our Empire, we now issue for a better understanding of Our intention the following decree which We hereby solemnly establish and order to be carried out to the full.

1. We permit all foreigners to come into Our Empire, in order to settle in all the governments, just as each one may desire.
2. After arrival, such foreigners can report for this purpose not only to the Guardianship Chancellery established for foreigners in our residence, but also, if more convenient, to the governor or commanding officer in one of the border-towns of the Empire.
3. Since those foreigners who would like to settle in Russia will also include some who do not have sufficient means to pay the required travel costs, they can report to our ministers in foreign courts, who will not only transport them to Russia at Our expense, but also provide them with travel money.
4. As soon as these foreigners arrive in our residence and report at the Guardianship Chancellery or in a border-town, they shall be required to state their true decision whether their real desire is to be enrolled in the guild of merchants or artisans, and become citizens, and in what city; or if they wish to settle on free, productive land in colonies and rural areas, to take up agriculture or some other useful occupation. Without delay, these people will be assigned to their destination, according to their own wishes and desires. From the following register* it can be seen in which regions of Our Empire free and suitable lands are still available. However, besides those listed, there are many more regions and all kinds of land where We will likewise permit people to settle, just as each one chooses for his best advantage.

*The register lists the areas where the immigrants can be settled.

St. Petersburg, 1756

5. Upon arrival in Our Empire, each foreigner who intends to become a settler and has reported to the Guardianship Chancellery or in other border-towns of Our Empire and, as already prescribed in # 4, has declared his decision, must take the oath of allegiance in accordance with his religious rite.
6. In order that the foreigners who desire to settle in Our Empire may realize the extent of Our benevolence to their benefit and advantage, this is Our will — :
    1. We grant to all foreigners coming into Our Empire the free and unrestricted practice of their religion according to the precepts and usage of their Church. To those, however, who intend to settle not in cities but in colonies and villages on uninhabited lands we grant the freedom to build churches and belltowers, and to maintain the necessary number of priests and church servants, but not the construction of monasteries. On the other hand, everyone is hereby warned not to persuade or induce any of the Christian co-religionists living in Russia to accept or even assent to his faith or join his religious community, under pain of incurring the severest punishment of Our law. This prohibition does not apply to the various nationalities on the borders of Our Empire who are attached to the Mahometan faith. We permit and allow everyone to win them over and make them subject to the Christian religion in a decent way.
    2. None of the foreigners who have come to settle in Russia shall be required to pay the slightest taxes to Our treasury, nor be forced to render regular or extraordinary services, nor to billet troops. Indeed, everybody shall be exempt from all taxes and tribute in the following manner: those who have been settled as colonists with their

families in hitherto uninhabited regions will enjoy 30 years of exemption; those who have established themselves, at their own expense, in cities as merchants and tradesmen in Our Residence St. Petersburg or in the neighboring cities of Livland, Esthonia, Ingermanland, Carelia and Finland, as well as in the Residential city of Moscow, shall enjoy 5 years of tax-exemption. Moreover, each one who comes to Russia, not just for a short while but to establish permanent domicile, shall be granted free living quarters for half a year.

3. All foreigners who settle in Russia either to engage in agriculture and some trade, or to undertake to build factories and plants will be offered a helping hand and the necessary loans required for the construction of factories useful for the future, especially of such as have not yet been built in Russia.

4. For the building of dwellings, the purchase of livestock needed for the farmstead, the necessary equipment, materials, and tools for agriculture and industry, each settler will receive the necessary money from our treasury in the form of an advance loan without any interest. The capital sum has to be repaid only after ten years, in equal annual instalments in the following three years.

5. We leave to the discretion of the established colonies and village the internal constitution and jurisdiction, in such a way that the persons placed in authority by Us will not interfere with the internal affairs and institutions. In other respects the colonists will be liable to our civil laws. However, in the event that the people would wish to have a special guardian or even an officer with a detachment of disciplined soldiers for the sake of security and defence, this wish would also be granted.

St. Petersburg, 1756

6. To every foreigner who wants to settle in Russia We grant complete duty-free import of his property, no matter what it is, provided, however, that such property is for personal use and need, and not intended for sale. However, any family that also brings in unneeded goods for sale will be granted free import on goods valued up to 300 rubles, provided that the family remains in Russia for at least 10 years. Failing which, it be required, upon its departure, to pay the duty both on the incoming and outgoing goods.
7. The foreigners who have settled in Russia shall not be drafted against their will into the military or the civil service during their entire stay here. Only after the lapse of the years of tax-exemption can they be required to provide labour service for the country. Whoever wishes to enter military service will receive, besides his regular pay, a gratuity of 30 rubles at the time he enrols in the regiment.
8. As soon as the foreigners have reported to the Guardianship Chancellery or to our border towns and declared their decision to travel to the interior of the Empire and establish domicile there, they will forthwith receive food rations and free transportation to their destination.
9. Those among the foreigners in Russia who establish factories, plants, or firms, and produce goods never before manufactured in Russia, will be permitted to sell and export freely for ten years, without paying export duty or excise tax.
10. Foreign capitalists who build factories, plants, and concerns in Russia at their own expense are permitted to purchase serfs and peasants needed for the operation of the factories.
11. We also permit all foreigners who have settled in colonies or villages to establish market days and annual

market fairs as they see fit, without having to pay any dues or taxes to our treasury.

7. All the afore-mentioned privileges shall be enjoyed not only by those who have come into our country to settle there, but also their children and descendants, even though these are born in Russia, with the provision that their years of exemption will be reckoned from the day their forebears arrived in Russia.

8. After the lapse of the stipulated years of exemption, all the foreigners who have settled in Russia are required to pay the ordinary moderate contributions and, like our other subjects, provide labor-service for their country. Finally, in the event that any foreigner who has settled in Our Empire and has become subject to Our authority should desire to leave the country, We shall grant him the liberty to do so, provided, however, that he is obligated to remit to Our treasury a portion of the assets he has gained in this country; that is, those who have been here from one to five years will pay one-fifth, whole [*sic*] those who have been here for five or more years will pay one-tenth. Thereafter each one will be permitted to depart unhindered anywhere he pleases to go.

9. If any foreigner desiring to settle in Russia wishes for certain reasons to secure other privileges or conditions besides those already stated, he can apply in writing or in person to our Guardianship Chancellery, which will report the petition to us. After examining the circumstances, We shall not hesitate to resolve the matter in such a way that the petitioner's confidence in Our love of justice will not be disappointed.

ST. PETERSBURG, 1756

> Given at the Court of Peter, July 22, 1763
> in the Second Year of Our Reign.
>
> The original was signed by Her Imperial Supreme Majesty's own hand.
>
> Printed by the Senate, July 25, 1763

Chapter 9

Go and Take Possession of the Good Land

"Always do what you are afraid to do." —Emerson

PETER HARDT READS THIS MANIFESTO with great interest. This is the break he has been waiting for. He applies in person to the Guardianship Chancellery, but is disappointed to be turned down, as only married couples will be allowed to take advantage of these land grants. The reason given is that unmarried women, not part of a family, could turn to prostitution to make a living. Unmarried men may also destabilize the moral fibre of communities. So, back at Zarskoje Selo, he languishes in his workers' quarters. Not much work is left to be done, and he has much idle time. He has saved most of his money and has banked a substantial amount with Ginsburg. He has become quite fond of Johanna Erlinger, but since the Storks returned to Germany, Johanna has been traveling a little here and there. Right now, he would be most appreciative of her company. She is a lovely-looking woman, quite intelligent, and a skilful jeweller, who has learned much from Aaron Stork about goldsmithery. She also used some of her savings to buy gold and jewels and makes beautiful jewellery when she is not working on the Amber Room. Additionally, she remodels older jewellery to her clients' requests. Some of her works fetch handsome amounts of money. Now that all work on the Amber Room is finished, she is probably in St. Petersburg or Moscow, selling her wares. She wants to make some money before her visa expires. Peter has not seen her for a few weeks, and he decides to visit Sergey and Esther. Since Esther's marriage to Sergey, his relationship with Esther has thawed a little, and he now has nothing more than a cordial relationship with the Ivanovs.

Esther and Sergey invite him to stay a few days so he can spend a little time in St. Petersburg and enjoy the sights. "So, what are you going to do Peter, now that the work in Zarskoje Selo is almost finished?" asks Sergey. Peter relates the news about his failed application for a land grant per the Catherine II manifesto.

Esther excitedly chimes in, "Johanna had the same experience. She was here yesterday—very disappointed. Now she has thoughts of returning to Germany, since her husband is no longer a threat to her, as you know. She has no children or relatives here. Aaron has suggested that she may work in his business back in Magdeburg."

Peter becomes quite upset and says, "Do you know where she is now?"

"No, Peter, but I would not be surprised if she is trying to book a passage in Kronstadt that takes her back to Germany."

"Why did she not say anything to me?" Peter questions. "How could she do such a thing?"

"Peter!" says Esther. "I must speak with you frankly. Johanna is a woman of some substance. She is well educated and well brought up. She has been in love with you ever since we arrived in Kronstadt all those years ago. She has wanted to tell you a thousand times that she was—is—in love with you. Did you not notice that? Where is your heart, Peter? Is it made of stone, like those that became the castle at Zarskoje Selo? Or did you expect her to fall at your feet, declare her love, and beg you to marry her and hope you accepted to save her dignity?"

Peter is stunned by this tirade. He cannot believe what an idiot he has been. He thought that Johanna would always be there and that when *he* was good and ready he could ask her to marry him.

"Then I shall make haste to see if I can find her there. Is there a coach that can take me there?" Peter becomes agitated.

"I'll take you there, Peter," Sergey offers generously. In a few minutes, they are on the way.

◊

In Kronstadt, Johanna is canvassing the various shipowner offices, but so far nothing is positive. On this hot August day, she decides to go to a quay restaurant to have a meal and a break from all that walking around in the hustle and bustle; she cuts an elegant but lonely figure in the crowd. Sergey, Esther, and Peter walk around to find her. Peter checks with the shipowners' offices, and they confirm that a woman fitting the description provided by Peter, has indeed been there that morning, but they have no idea where she might be now. Peter is a little happier at that news, as there is a good chance he will find her here. He picks up the pace and almost begins running.

Esther suggests that they eat something before resuming their search. They locate a nice restaurant near the water and order their lunches. As they eat, Esther has that same feeling she had on the ship shortly after they left Lübeck, that someone is watching her. She mentions it to Peter, who looks behind him but sees no one whom he recognizes. Still, Esther insists that someone is watching them. Peter lifts his head and looks straight ahead. Through the open door that leads to the alfresco area, a pair of eyes bores into Peter. His heart leaps into his throat and pounds wildly. Johanna has been observing them for a little while. Peter jumps up and races toward Johanna, almost sending a waiter and his tray flying. He embraces her, and they both burst into tears.

On the way back in the coach, Peter proposes to Johanna, who is delighted to accept his offer of marriage. Esther and Sergey give them their blessing. Until their marriage, Johanna is welcome to stay with Esther and Sergey while Peter winds up his work in Zarskoje Selo.

Immediately after their marriage, they both apply to the Guardianship Chancellery for the land grant. This time, they are successful. However they must wait a little while, as Russia is expecting a mass influx of migrants who wish to take advantage of this offer. Once a good number are approved and categorized by their religion and place of origin, they will be taken to their respective portions of land. Meanwhile, Peter and Johanna rent an apartment not far from Joachim and Elisabeth. Peter is making architectural plans for his house and the smithy that he will build. He has looked at a number of forges and noted their good features and where he would improve. Johanna continues designing and making jewellery, which she sells to the upmarket shops in St. Petersburg.

The only person of the Group of Seven who is well settled in Russia is Esther, since her marriage to Sergey gave her permanent residency, as well as Russian citizenship. The greatest threat is for Elisabeth and Joachim. They would love to stay in St. Petersburg, but their visas will not be renewed under the present circumstances, especially since they are both registered as Jews. Although the manifesto makes reference to freedom of religion, in practice, that does not apply to Jews. The only real option is to apply for a land grant under the manifesto. They do have a little money, and Esther has given them the house at 30 Kazanskaya Ulitska. The value of the house is around 16,500 rubles. With such money, they could establish themselves well with a land grant near Saratov. Esther is a little sad that they may have to part with Joachim and Elisabeth, but consoles herself with the fact that they can probably visit once a year.

Before the manifesto comes into full effect, it takes a while for the mass arrivals of "hopefuls" who want to take advantage of their new opportunity. Then, in 1766, Tsarina Catherine the Great officially grants "freedom of worship" to all Russians and immigrants. This is the cue for Joachim and Elisabeth.

Massive boatloads of migrants arrive at Oranienbaum, near St. Petersburg. Many come on the pink *Slon*, the same ship that brought the Group of Seven to Russia. Compared with the group's passage from Lübeck in 1755, these new immigrants do not have such a comfortable trip. Now the boats are hugely overloaded and the conditions are cramped and unhygienic. Consequently, many do not make it to Russia alive but are buried unceremoniously at sea. Upon their arrival, it becomes abundantly clear that they are second-class migrants in comparison with those who arrived at the invitation of the crown or who came here on business years earlier. Kuhlberg is still in charge, only the immigrants' papers are not so well "documented" as Esther's were. In addition, these newcomers must undergo a process of "Russification." For up to two months, they learn basic Russian, about Russian laws and regulations, and about government and tradition, and take an oath of allegiance to the Russian crown. Although the manifesto seems to allow the immigrants to retain their language and culture, the real intention is to absorb them into the Russian way of life. They all receive a small allowance of rubles. Before their departure to take possession of their land, they need to buy necessary winter clothing and household goods to get them started. Two months after the first loads of migrants arrive; a group is assembled for departure. Peter and Johanna travel with this first group. All of the members are from Hessia in Germany, many from Offenbach. Peter knows a few from when he lived in Offenbach. They understand each other well, as they all speak the Hessian dialect, which provides a form of identity for the group. Peter and Johanna are probably the best-prepared couple in the group. They have a much better command of the Russian language and understanding of the Russian culture. For this reason, many see Peter and Johanna as their guides and protectors. As a group, however, they know little about their destination only that it is near the city of Saratov, down the Volga River. A number of the group are already disgruntled over the fact that they believed that they could choose where to settle, whereas Kuhlberg strongly "persuaded" them to get into this "Saratov party"—"if you know what is good for you," he said threateningly in German. And with his heavy Russian accent, it sounded very menacing indeed.

Kuhlberg bluntly told any tradesmen among the group that they have to be farmers. Peter and Johanna, who have come on their terms, under provisions of the manifesto, may establish their business with the forge, as Peter has planned. Of course, they need to do farm work if they want to survive and stay in the framework of the manifesto. However, if the group thinks that the journey thus far is bad and this trip to Saratov disappointing, they are in for a rude shock at what awaits them.

Chapter 10

A Troubled Paradise

"Pain and pleasure are simply ideas incapable of definition." —Burke

THE JOURNEY BEGINS WITH TWENTY horse-drawn covered wagons. Twelve of the wagons are loaded with the adventurous migrants' personal effects. One wagon carries all the camping gear, which will have to be unpacked each night, as well as all the food and cooking utensils for making their meals. The first leg of their seven-hundred-kilometre journey is to Moscow. The first few days and nights are bearable, but this kind of traveling brings with it its share of frustration and mistrust. The late summer makes the traveling and sleeping uncomfortable. Irritations because of lack of sleep, mosquitoes, roaming bears, or annoyance with one another's habits and the mixing up of personal items seem to be the most common failings. The group leaders have their work cut out to keep a positive spirit among the group. Peter and Johanna are wondering what they are in for. Nevertheless, they are determined to see this through, and since both of them are not pessimists they encourage each other with their grand plans. Indeed, that is what most of the conversations on the wagons and around the night-time campfires are about. All of them have their own picture of their piece of "paradise."

Moscow is a nice break from the arduous journey. There is time to look around the city and to replenish food supplies and buy other items they have learned will be necessary before they begin the second leg, from Moscow to Saratov, a trip of around 850 kilometres. That journey seems to go on forever. Peter starts to have serious misgivings about their decision to join this group, but Johanna is far more optimistic. She continues to make plans with Peter. Given the time of the year, they hope to arrive at their destination soon so that they can start building and preparing the fields. They already know something about the Russian winter, but even *they* will be in for a surprise.

First, however, they arrive at Saratov, which eventually will be their nearest major city. They are relieved to see a reasonable-size city with all the essential goods and services available. Peter takes the opportunity to purchase essential equipment for the forge, like hammers, bellows, sacks of coal, an anvil, horseshoes, and a quantity of steel. The group also purchases saws and tools of various kinds, as well as nails. Peter is pleased with his equipment, but the wagons groan under the extra weight. "But how far out of the city will our land be?" they all ask. They are soon to find out.

Two days later, they leave the city at dawn, heading east. Then they arrive at the mighty Volga River. "What are we doing here?" Peter asks the leader of the group.

"We are doing nothing here. We are crossing over the river on the punt, one wagon at a time," he says in his heavy Russian accent. The Volga is two kilometers wide at this point. Once across, the wagons continue for two and a half days in a north-easterly direction, and then they stop. "Why are we setting up camp? It is not night-time," someone shouts.

"On the contrary," says the leader, "this is where you will camp—permanently." He lets out a raucous laugh.

✦

They are all shocked and disbelieving when the leader tells them to unload the wagons, for this is where they are to start a new life. Except for a few patches of forest, the land is flat, with one-meter-high grass as far as the eye can see. The land assigned to them is just a wide tract of uncultivated steppe, populated sparsely by some rough, nomadic, semi savage tribes, predominantly Tartars, Bashkirs, Kalmucks, and Kirkiz. This side of the Volga is called the *Wiesenseite*—a nice-sounding name meaning "meadow side of the Volga," yet it is anything but a meadow.

Those with agricultural experience can see the potential but as yet have not experienced the seasons and weather conditions under which they will work, nor do they understand the quality of the soil. So everything is a new experience. Nearby runs a small river that eventually becomes a tributary to the Volga River. The group leaders apportion the land in thirty-hectare allotments. Thus, one of the first things for the men to do is to peg out the boundaries. If there was any squabbling among the group on the journey, it is no more. The reality of the situation calls for unity and cooperation among all. Peter galvanizes the group into action. His architectural mind is one of organization and structure. He has already assessed the skills of the men in the group and now makes good use of their abilities. He counts saw millers, carpenters, cabinetmakers, miners, farmers, hunters, seamstresses, tailors, bakers, butchers, stonemasons, and one midwife, plus Peter's own blacksmith and architectural skills and Johanna's jewellery and bookkeeping abilities. Peter also has some medical training from his uncle Alexander in Frankfurt. All in all, there seem to be enough skills to form a viable community and support for one another.

Peter begins assigning jobs and setting some basic regulations. All must camp in close proximity to one another for safety's sake. Those men who own a musket and who have butchering experience will hunt for elk and pig to provide meat. Males sixteen years and older are organized into working gangs. The twenty wagons are for the entire group's use. One team goes to cut timber. Another group is assigned to process the timber. Still others are to clear the land. The younger boys go and collect wood for the cooking. The women prepare the food and will start working the land as soon some of the older boys have tilled it with horse and plows. Some fields are soon ready to plant a winter crop. This is a basic survival plan, and all are eager to do their share.

The warm weather is still holding in early September, but the sky is looking ominous. Peter quickly designs a large shelter for all forty families in case the weather changes. But while it is still warm enough to work and sleep outside, the shelter becomes the timber mill and storage for goods. A second shelter is soon erected to accommodate people and the cooking facilities. Some forty log cabins begin to take shape along a primitive road that services the entire community. The weather becomes decidedly cooler as families move into their cabins to begin some normality of life. Those with carpentry skills construct beds, chairs, tables, and outdoor toilets. Two wagons with four men are dispatched to return to Saratov to buy potbellied stoves and ovens. They also need bedding and warm *doonas* (duvets). Peter and another three men are on the way to Krasny Kut, a little farther south, where some Russians settled as farmers ten years ago. to negotiate the sale of some cows and a bull. The Russians drive a hard bargain, but eventually they agree on a price, along with a few bottles of vodka. The men return with several pigs, chickens, ducks, and turkeys. The hamlet begins to look like a proper farming community, with farmyards that have stables for their animals. These are now securely fenced in.

Peter's plan for the community is to have in place all the basic structures for surviving the savage winter. A group effort is necessary to dig a well for the hamlet to have access to fresh water. In winter it will be too risky to go to the creek for it. They complete this task by the middle of October. The men are totally exhausted from the long hours they have worked since they arrived here, but now they are ready and prepared, and a measure of pride in their accomplishments is clearly visible on their faces.

Peter and all the people of the hamlet then gather to celebrate what they have achieved in these two months. They open a few bottles of vodka for the occasion, and Peter gives a speech to thank them all for their fine cooperation and to express his wishes to continue as a community. "However, it is now important that we come to have a proper name. I propose that we call this hamlet by a name from our own area in Hessia. If you will all agree, we shall henceforth be known as the people from Enders." Spontaneous applause seals this inaugural ceremony. "In the spring of next year, 1767, we will be officially registered as a village belonging to the district of Saratov."

Then a young man brings out his "squeezebox" and plays a few folk tunes from "home," and they all sing and dance in the street. A lot of the disappointments and heartache are forgotten, and a new spirit invigorates the men and women. A few of the women are in their early stages of pregnancy and are registering their details with the midwife, Anna, a kindly, experienced woman. Anna and Johanna also double as the village registrars and gazetteers for the time being, so that all is accounted for when needed.

※

The winter of 1766–67 is indeed savage. Temperatures drop to negative forty-five degrees Celsius at night, and warm by only a few degrees during the day. Wolves continually harass the hamlet to get some of the livestock. They are also a threat to the people. Many feel uneasy in this environment and are fearful of the wolves. In the winter, there is not much to do in the fields. The womenfolk knit furiously to keep the families in warm socks and jumpers. There is a lot of work to do on their homes and to look after the livestock. For Peter, it is a welcome change from the many duties he performed to establish this hamlet. He now concentrates on building his forge from the plans he made. Johanna is pleased to have a little time for her jewellery work, which she hopes to sell in the spring next year in Saratov.

Very astutely, some of the men begin to study the wolves' behavior. In this way, they learn to live among wolves—both real wolves and the wolf-like behaviors of the nomadic men who appear from time to time to spy on the villagers. The villagers pass on their knowledge to the community. However, since children are most vulnerable because of their naïveté, older women with a yen for telling stories to their children find wolves to be a great subject. To instil respect and caution, if not fear of wolves, they soon develop a plethora of exaggerated stories about wolves that can give some children nightmares. However, there is also time for the children to be schooled in reading, writing, and basic mathematics. German is the official and well-guarded language in the region, yet parents realize that the children also need to learn Russian. Hence, Peter and Johanna are temporarily the teachers of this subject.

Another skill that the community of Enders quickly learns and shares is the art of distilling vodka from potatoes. Peter has purchased a crude still from the Russian farmers at Karpenka, a village near Krasny Kut, along with instructions on how to use it, and others are copying the stills. However, since potatoes are still a scarce commodity this winter, only a few have allowed themselves the luxury of making vodka. They are hoping for a good harvest next year, so they keep most of the potatoes for seedlings.

Peter, who soon receives the nickname Schulz (Mayor), forms a counsel of the men to plan the development and the protection of the village. There is a need for night watchmen, and a roster for all to share in this duty. Schooling needs to be organized for the children, but as yet no one is available as a teacher. A central baking oven is urgently needed and will be built under the supervision of the only baker, Johannes Kramer, and the two stonemasons, Friedrich Berger and his brother, Thomas. This oven will be built on the eastern side of the proposed village square. This square will also serve as the central gathering place of all the villagers in cases of emergency, which will be invoked by the ringing of the bell in the bell tower situated in the square. And, although Peter is a nominal Mennonite, the village will be registered as "Evangelical"—that is,

A Troubled Paradise

Protestant—and a small church will be built by this time next year, as a community project. It is decided that those men with specialized skills, such as butcher and baker, should apprentice some of the younger men to teach them these essential skills for the survival of the community. Such instruction should be reserved for winter, when there is little agricultural work to be done. Finally, there is the question of postal service. It is decided that every month, a designated person will take mail to Saratov and require the postal service to hold any mail for collection once a month. This latter decision is greeted with much relief, as in the depressing winter, the women in particular become quite homesick when left to their own thoughts. Writing to their relatives in Germany and receiving some news from them would definitely lift their spirits. Anna and Johanna note these decisions and place them on a notice board in the village square.

Amid all this planning, the winter passes quickly—that is, in the calendar. However, spring does not occur here, as the folks were used to in Germany. Winter, ice and snow, and wolves and bears remain a problem for another two months. Then, suddenly, the air warms and the snow melts, creating a slushy mess on the ground for days. The air grows warmer by the day, and all are on standby to start the agricultural work. Everyone in the family is assigned a job; the plows are in the fields, tilling the ground and preparing it for seeding. The still-moist soil and the increasing heat produce a bumper crop of wheat and rye, while the gardens around the home begin flourishing with vegetables. Fruit trees are bought and planted. The whole village resembles an ants' nest.

The steady arrival of masses of wagons with immigrants punctuates the hive of activity in the village. Many who are settling in this region come to look at Enders. They have been informed that this is a model village, and some of the newcomers wish to speak with the families here about what to do to set up their own villages and benefit from the families' experiences, albeit very limited. One group is so impressed with Peter Hardt's organizational structure that they settle in close proximity to Enders and called their new village by Peter's nickname, Schulz. Another group settles a little farther east and calls their village Urbach. Thus, a whole string of villages springs up in the next few years from Mariental to the Volga, and then, going north, many more villages and cities are founded. The people in the whole region become known as *Die Wolga Deutschen* (the Volga Germans). Within a few years, some sixty thousand people, predominantly Germans, are living in this area, producing large crops and creating an economy all their own. The exemption from tax and military service gives the settlers a basis to build up their wealth.

One afternoon during the late summer of 1767, Peter and Johanna have just come in from the fields and Johanna is preparing the evening meal, when there is a knock on the door. A young, handsome couple stand there, smiling at Johanna. Johanna's eyes open wide, and she wants to let out an excited scream, but she covers her mouth and runs back inside. "Peter, Peter, quick—we have visitors and you will not believe who they are."

Peter rushes to the door and sees the large frame of Joachim Hahn and his wife, Elisabeth. They greet each other with hugs and kisses and much joy. Elisabeth notes the bulge on Johanna's belly. "Oh, Johanna, what a great joy to see you again, and you are expecting. Guess what?" Elisabeth almost whispers. "So am I." The two women hug each other again.

"Come inside, and let us talk," says Peter. Once they are all settled, Johanna gets dinner ready with Elisabeth by her side, chatting away about the days when they were together in Zarskoje Selo and, of course, babies.

Peter pours himself and Joachim a cup of vodka. "So, what gives us the honor of your visit?" Peter inquires.

"Elisabeth and I have just arrived and want to settle in Urbach."

Peter and Johanna are very excited to hear this news. "Please, Joachim, let us help you settle in Urbach. You can stay with us for a little while until you build your home, and we are happy to help you build," Peter offers.

Joachim tries to politely dissuade Peter, but to no avail. "Well, then, Peter, we accept your generous offer. I want to build a small cottage for us, and a workshop where I can make wagons."

"You will be in great demand," Peter says. "With the rapid growth of Urbach and the surrounding villages, you will be inundated with work. Maybe when I am rich I can buy one of your lovely coaches," he jokes.

"Perhaps I can help you set up your forge here in Enders in return for your generous assistance," Joachim offers.

"Cooperation is the survival password for all of us in this vulnerable environment," Peter adds, with a fatherly touch on Joachim's broad shoulders. "Good muscles there, lad!"

Joachim and Elisabeth stay with the Hardts while Joachim does some repairs on several wagons that the villagers will need for their harvest. Then they begin the work of building their home in Urbach and start cultivating the land.

In the Urbach region, the harvest of the late summer of 1767 is incredibly hard work. No one anticipates that the reduced time frame for bringing in all the produce demands that the men often sleep in the fields to save time traveling, while the womenfolk remain in the homesteads, looking after the little ones They take care of the animals, prepare and preserve foodstuffs, make vodka, bake bread, and, of course, gossip, their favorite pastime. While all this paints a gloriously rustic picture, a dreadful danger lurks from an unsuspected source, and causes some rethinking of the villages' security.

❖

Johanna and Elisabeth have become close friends. Johanna often stays a few days with Elisabeth when Peter comes to have work done on a wagon. Peter also helps Joachim with some late harvesting work in the fields. It happens on one of these visits, during a late-summer evening, that the bell tower suddenly begins ringing the signal of danger. Johanna stops cooking the food for the men for the next day and listens intently. She hears the screams of young women coming from the northern end of the village.

Suddenly, Elisabeth bursts through the front door and shouts, "Hide yourself, Johanna, and barricade the doors! We are being raided!"

"Who is raiding us?"

"I don't know. Just hurry." Elisabeth slams the steel bars across the back and front doors and grabs Johanna by the hand, and through a concealed back door they rush out into the workshop, where there are good hiding places. A rogue group of the rough, nomadic, semi savage Kirkiz tribe are storming into Urbach on their horses, raiding the village for vodka and salted meats, and raping some of the women. Johanna and Elisabeth, both of whom are pregnant, hide in the workshop. The Kirkizers, as the village people have begun to call them, rush into Joachim's property and try to force open the doors. Peter has built very strong metal bars on the doors for Joachim and instructed Elisabeth well on how to secure the doors and windows. The Kirkizers begin to scream and bash the doors and windows in frustration. Then they move toward the workshop. The women's hearts almost stop as they see four fierce-looking men checking the area of the forge. Johanna and Elisabeth crouch even lower to the ground in their hiding place. The men stand almost over them. Their alcohol breath permeates the forge. Suddenly they leave, cursing, as they do not think they might find women or vodka in a forge.

The two women stay there for what seems an eternity, before they dare to move out of the workshop, but with great caution; then they go quickly into the house to clean themselves up. They are still shaking when Joachim, Peter, and the other men working in the fields arrive after hearing the bell tower.

The next day, the full horror of the raid becomes clear. One young man of this group became so ambitious and testosterone driven that he went rampaging into several houses on his own. He saw a fifteen-year-old girl cowering in a corner of her bedroom. He rushed over to her as she screamed in terror. He ripped her dress apart and threw her violently on the bed, then climbed on top of her. As he kissed her, his vile vodka breath and the shock of the attack suddenly made her vomit all over him. He jumped up in horror and then began to hit her with his strong fist. Suddenly, he slumped down with an almighty groan his eyes wide open. Blood was running out of his mouth.

As the girl looked up, her mother stood there, petrified. She had been hiding with a large butcher's knife behind the bedroom curtain. When she could not bear it any longer, she crept up behind the man and stabbed him in the heart from behind. He died on the bedroom floor. The raid was quickly reported to the men in the fields, who rushed back to the village. The rest of the raiders fled, to hide and wait for another opportunity. However, from the dead man, and the group's Mongolian facial features and clothing, the villagers were able to establish that these men were indeed Kirkizers.

The raid causes an enormous outburst of anger among all the villages. It also causes a great conflict of interest, between pursuing the men and bringing in the harvest. There is precious little time for either. Yet the outraged women demand justice. So the men quickly decide to erect a pole in the village square and nail the corpse to it. They gather some wood, and, before burning the object of their abhorrence, the women file past the man and spit on him.

That satisfies the women, but there is now a big threat looming. So the village counsellors urgently gather to form a plan for security in the summer months. They fear revenge from the Kirkizers for the murder of one of theirs. It is decided that each village will have six armed guards remain behind to protect the village and the women, who, understandably, are feeling vulnerable. The guards from each village will rotate on a weekly roster basis. They will also be responsible for all other security measures or unrests.

Still, the raids of the Kirkiz, Tartars, Kalmucks, and Bashkirs continue periodically in this region. They seem to target villages that have few men left to defend them. In some instances, when they come in large numbers, they completely destroy a village and enslave the people by deporting them. But besides the obvious legacy of pregnancies from the Kirkizer raids, which leaves as a visual reminder, the incident of the raid in Enders is put to rest. A consensus is reached that the children fathered by the Kirkizers will not be discriminated against and will have the full rights of family and community. However, a number of the villages request military security, as Catherine II promised in her manifesto but which has not happened yet. Consequently, as the settlers have already experienced, what the manifesto states and what occurs in reality are different things.

Much like the exaggerated stories about wolves, a number of tales develop about the Kirkizers. These are handed down from generation to generation with the appropriate embellishments, such as "The Kirkizers and the Kalmucks are *so* ugly; they have only one eye. When you look at one, you will shudder with horror." Whatever the stories are, they serve as a cautionary tale to the next generation to be on guard. And the next generation does not take long to come.

One of the happy bits of news that Peter sends from Enders to his parents in Offenbach is that Johanna has given birth to twin boys, named Gottlieb and Phillip, born on October 12, 1767. Joachim and Elisabeth quickly visit Enders to share in the joy of the birth of their twins. Other children are born, and Anna the midwife is kept busy. Livestock is also increasing through husbandry breeding and purchases. Johanna and Anna also take much care to chronicle the birth of the children and all events that are taking place. Every month, they or someone designated by them travels to Saratov to register the births of the children. Meanwhile, Elisabeth, in Urbach, gives birth to a boy on February 19, 1768, whom they name Aaron in honor of the child's grandfather, who now lives in Magdeburg, Germany.

Each year, here and in all the nearby villages, the harvest is brought in with much rejoicing. In Enders, Peter and the counsellors set up a village festival called *Erntedankfest* to thank God for the harvest. Potatoes will also be harvested soon, and that means vodka will be flowing in the winter months. At this time, the villagers also slaughter some of their pigs and butcher them, preserving pork meat in drums laced with salt, making sausages, brawn, and whatever else they can make from a pig. They have already finely chopped their cabbages and placed them into wooden barrels, pressed down tightly, each layer salted generously. When the barrel is full, they put a lid on it with a heavy stone holding it down and leave it standing for four months. Thus, the traditional pork and sauerkraut with potatoes is a featured dish around this joyful time. Afterward, they will again prepare the fields for the winter crops, and so the cycle of life and living continues, among all sorts of troublesome "wolves."

✦

The snow this winter is particularly deep. The huge increase in population and animals is straining the environment to cope with sanitation. Little do they suspect that under this beautiful snow lies a deadly enemy. What this is will be revealed when the snow melts in April/May. When it does, the streets and yards are particularly slushy and carry mud to the doors of the dwellings. The melting waters that run like small rivers carry with them all the animal dung, human excrement from the toilets, and dead animals, which pollute the drinking water in the well. In this environment the bacterium *Vibrio cholerae* becomes a deadly plague.

Unsuspectingly, the cholera virus also enters the homes of the villagers on the hands and feet of infected people.

The first sign of any problem comes when the Baker family call Anna to have a look at their baby daughter, who is lying down sick. She is rapidly dehydrating and vomiting and has severe diarrhea. Her hands are wrinkly and her eyes are sunken. Anna calls Peter to have a look too. He orders everyone to wash his or her hands in hot water. After looking at the baby, Anna and Peter come to the conclusion that it is indeed the cholera plague.

The village bell sounds a dull, regular beat, something that everyone dreads. A small coffin is carried out of the Bakers' house and taken to slightly higher ground that has been set aside for the cemetery. A little cross over the mound of soggy earth reads JULIANNA MEYER—BORN APRIL 22, 1768, DIED MAY 4, 1769. They bury her there as the first person to die in Enders, but she will not be the last victim of this plague.

Within a short period of four weeks, the cemetery has twenty-eight graves. The village is demoralized by the continuous ringing of the bell and the desperate cries of loved ones who are losing someone dear and close to them. The cholera also ravages Urbach and bereaves families of children, as well as parents. A number are left orphaned. Peter and Johanna, who take immediate sanitary precautions and are spared from the plague, adopt one of these children, a little four-year-old girl. Her name is Rosanna.

Thus, with the cholera plagues and the raids, some seven thousand people perish in the 104 villages along the Volga River within the first decade of settlements. For example, the nearby village of Rosenheim's population alone drops from 251 to 226 by 1769, despite a rapid birth rate.

In the wake of this plague come the tasks of working the fields with a reduced labor force. No family is left to struggle on its own, so the men work very hard and long hours to see the villages through to the harvest. Additionally, Anna and Johanna must support the grieving families and widows. Many of them want to

A Troubled Paradise

return to Germany but realize that they are stuck here. The two women arrange to ensure proper care for these people's physical, emotional, and spiritual needs. Some of the new villages, initially, are spared the plague in its first spring thaw. However, the devastation of this plague in the more established villages serves as a caution to the new villages not to be complacent about their sanitation. While this advice is gratefully accepted, in practice that is not always possible. Manure from horses and cows is carefully gathered to fertilize the fields, but other excrement is still left on the ground, and the outhouse toilets are a concern in this matter. Hence, each succeeding spring the cholera plague makes its grim appearance, claiming a number of victims, mostly the very young. Only the hardiest babies are tough enough to survive. The most vulnerable are the ones born in the middle of winter, who are only between one and four months old when the thaw begins and brings with it the threat of cholera. In Urbach, the habit develops of dipping newborns in ice-cold water immediately after their birth. After the ice in a village well is broken, the water is drawn in a wooden bucket and the baby is dunked in it. If it survives, it is deemed strong and hardy. If it dies in the process, then it is deemed weak. It is a bizarre measure for bizarre times.

In the wake of all this tragedy comes another major disruption to the development of the villages: the Cossack Rebellion of 1773/5. These Cossacks, under the leadership of Pugachev, from the Ukraine region, resent their takeover by the Russian government. As they mount attacks and raids on Russian principalities, they often cross into the *Wolga Deutschen* area. They do so not with the intention of targeting the villagers' properties or lives; nevertheless, the Cossacks do some damage to the property and settlers, and the frequent raids make the men apprehensive and the women fearful of being raped—and for good reason. Some of the more testosterone-driven Cossacks see in these defenceless people an opportunity to satisfy their sexual urges. They also have a deep loathing for Jews and thus target any Jewish settlements. However, these incidents are rare.

◈

Although Esther thought that she and Sergey could visit Joachim in Urbach every year, which proves to be far more optimistic than practical. Nevertheless, through correspondence they keep in touch and up to date. However, Esther needs to see her son, her daughter-in-law, and her now three grandsons, Aaron, Jacob, and Itzhak. So she sets aside the summer of 1781 to visit Urbach. Sergey and Esther have retired from the orchestra the previous year and can now plan for this event.

The trip is pleasant in parts but arduous in others. When they reach Enders and Urbach, they are pleasantly surprised by the civic pride of the villages, which are well organized and cared for. In Urbach, there are a few businesses and shops set up by the local Jewish community to cater to the needs of the growing population. This forms the core of a small Jewish enclave in Urbach. Trees planted over a decade ago line the main street. It is hard for Sergey and Esther to imagine the bland landscape Joachim and Elisabeth have described existing when they first arrived here.

The reunion is a most joyous occasion. Esther and Sergey bring presents for the family. Esther is a little overcome when she hugs her grandchildren and holds little Itzhak in her arms. She seems so fulfilled. Joachim proudly shows Sergey his well-established workshop and two coaches that he is building. There are also two new wagons in the yard, ready to be picked up for the upcoming harvest. However, his pride and joy are his horses. There are six in his stables, a very strong and healthy breed. Joachim has also learned from Peter the basics of running a forge, mostly to shoe the horses, his own and others in the village. During the previous winter, Joachim made some plaster molds from his bronze insignia and learned to replicate them. Sergey is suitably impressed.

A Troubled Paradise

"Do you like our home?" Elisabeth asks as she shows it to her mother-in-law.

"Elisabeth, this is so cozy and very tastefully decorated. You must have invested a lot of your money into setting yourselves up with such a good home and business," Esther compliments Elisabeth. The log cabin that was their first home is still standing and is used to house their chickens and ducks. Their new home is very well constructed, with four bedrooms, all nicely furnished.

"Joachim is such a good worker with timber; he seems to really love it. He made the tables and chairs, as well as the beds," Elisabeth says with great pride, running her fingers over the smooth surface of the furniture.

Esther observes Elisabeth as she displays the home. She seems a little tired from running the business, the house, and the farm and looking after three boys. Esther is pleased to help out with the cooking and looking after the boys, while Sergey helps Joachim get the place ready for the harvest. However, Esther and Sergey are starting to feel the drain of advancing years, and their energy is not as plentiful as it used to be. Esther is worried for Elisabeth and mentions it to her.

"Oh, please don't worry. I am all right. You have met the lovely Stampe family, our Jewish neighbors? The mother and her daughter, Anne, often come and help out with work when it gets to be too much for me. In return, Joachim teaches their son some of the woodworking crafts."

"Well, just take good care of yourself—the boys need their mother," Esther says in her maternal voice.

Esther finds the opportunity to speak with Joachim alone. "Joachim, my dear son, Sergey and I are getting older and life will not go on forever for any of us. We have to be practical about these things. Sergey and I are quite well off and will leave everything to you in our will. There is a lawyer in St. Petersburg who will contact you if need be. However, I have learned from life experiences that you cannot totally trust people. So I have hidden in our bedroom some items that are very personal to us. You will have to look for them. They are between the wood panelling and the wall. The only way you can find them is by tapping the panels. The one that is movable has a higher pitch, but it does not move easily."

Joachim is a little disturbed by his mother's talk of death. He cannot contemplate such an eventuality. However he is realistic enough to know that this must come one day and so he assures his mother that he will look after her belongings, but begs her to take good care of herself and Sergey.

Then, before the harvest begins, they take their leave and return to St. Petersburg via Enders, where they will stay a few days with Peter and Johanna.

Eight months later a sombre-looking letter with a black edge is hand-delivered to Esther in St. Petersburg. She has a bad feeling about it. As she looks at the sender—*Joachim Hahn, Urbach Kr. Saratov*—she lays the letter aside. Later, when Sergey comes home, she asks him to open it, which he does. However, since it is written in German, he hands it back to Esther to read. She reads it sentence by sentence and translates it for Sergey.

Dearest Mother,
My heart breaks as I write this letter to you and Sergey to inform you that my dear little boy Itzhak died in the cholera plague this spring. It is hard to describe the pain that I feel and that I saw on the face of my lovely Elisabeth. I can hardly imagine what she must have experienced over the death of her little boy. She refused to be comforted or to even eat a little. I worried for her health. I called the rabbi to speak with her, but she was angry with God that he took her son, so she refused any comfort from him. Then suddenly she took ill with cholera and she died within two days. This double loss is unbearable for me. Aaron and Jacob cannot comprehend why their mother is not with us anymore, just as I did not fully comprehend it

when Papa died; I only carried with me this awful feeling for years. That is how the boys must feel now. Oh, Mother, now I can understand what you must have felt that day in the Judengasse in Frankfurt when you received the news that Papa had died.

Elisabeth was such a good wife. She had great hopes and plans for us here in Urbach. Now I will have to continue living here without her, but she wants me to succeed. This she told me before she died. "Please take care of the boys" were her last words before she slipped away.

Please don't worry. I am strong and will survive. I shall throw myself into my work to fulfill Elisabeth's dreams and raise our boys here. Our neighbors the Stampe family are very helpful in these difficult days by taking care of the boys.

I love you, Mother. Give my greetings to Sergey.
Your son,
Joachim

Esther is heartbroken as she falls into Sergey's arms and sobs. They both feel totally helpless. Nothing has prepared them for this eventuality. Neither their Eastern Orthodox religion nor Esther's Jewish beliefs provide any comfort. Sergey, who lost his wife and child, can deeply empathize with Esther and Joachim's losses, but he also is unable to come to terms with untimely deaths.

Some days later, when they are warming themselves in front of a cozy fire and sipping a glass of port, Esther tells Sergey of the letter that Itzhak sent her before he died, in which he expressed some surprising faith in a resurrection to the paradise here on Earth. "Itzhak seemed to derive deep comfort from this Bible teaching, and so did I at the time," says Esther thoughtfully.

Sergey is intrigued by this thought. As he ponders it, a great calm comes over him. "Esther," he says, reaching for her hand, "I also find this most comforting." They snuggle up to each other without saying any more. Peace has returned to their hearts. The next day, Esther writes to Joachim and mentions the same biblical thought to him, in the hope that he, too, may find "the peace of

God which surpasses all understanding," which she quotes from the Bible.

✧

Anne Margrete Stampe, who is twelve years Joachim's junior, becomes the stabilizing factor in the lives of Joachim and his boys. She is an extremely capable young woman. Some eighteen months have passed since Elisabeth died, and Joachim is falling in love with Anne. He writes to his mother expressing his feelings for Anne, but he has misgivings about marrying her so soon after Elisabeth has died. When he receives his mother's reply, she urges him to make a life for himself and the boys. *They need a mother, Joachim*, she writes, *and you are still young and you need a wife. Marry her; you have our blessing.* So, on December 20, 1784, the rabbi marries them in Urbach. In time, she gives birth to a daughter, Anne Catherine, and a son, Karl Joseph.

✧

In the summer of 1787, rumors are running around the villages that Her Imperial Majesty Catherine II the Great is going to visit the Crimea, as unrests have started to disturb that region. Her Majesty also plans to inspect a number of the German villages on the way. Great excitement sets in when these rumors are officially confirmed. Among the chosen villages is Urbach. When Her Imperial Majesty and all her entourage arrive in Urbach, all the men, women, and children are neatly dressed in traditional Hessian costumes and line the main street. In the village square is a large wooden sign, carved in German, with the words YOUR IMPERIAL MAJESTY! WELCOME TO URBACH, THE HESSIA OF THE RUSSIAN EMPIRE. The ornate sign is embellished with many brightly colored carved roses. The addition of the word *HESSIA* is in honor of Her

Imperial Majesty's origins in Hessia, Germany. The other Urbach, in Germany, is well known to her too.

When the Tsarina sees the sign, she orders the coaches to stop. Escorted, she walks over to the sign and asks in German, "Who made this beautiful sign?"

One village elder steps forward, bows, and says, "Your Imperial Majesty! Our coachbuilder, Mr. Joachim Hahn, made this sign in your honor."

"Ask him to come here," she says benignly.

Joachim steps forward and says, "Your Imperial Majesty!" and bows to the Tsarina.

"Where did you learn to do such beautiful work?"

"From the coachbuilder Vladimir Zázvorková in St. Petersburg, ma'am, who learned the trade from my grandfather in Ludwigsburg."

"I am familiar with Mr. Zázvorková. And your father?"

"He died in Frankfurt, ma'am. Mother immigrated to Russia in 1756 and settled in St. Petersburg."

"And what does your mother do in St. Petersburg, may I ask?"

"Mother married Sergey Ivanov, conductor of the St. Petersburg orchestra. She was the concertmaster of the orchestra. They are both now retired."

"Well, well, Mr. Ivanov!" the Tsarina exclaims. "I know that gentlemen very well, and in that case, I have met your mother also. What a happy coincidence. Bless you, my son," she says, and makes the sign of the cross in front of Joachim's face. Joachim feels extremely uncomfortable with this gesture by the Tsarina. However, he does not show it, but bows graciously and thanks the Tsarina, who offers her hand to Joachim as a farewell gesture, before boarding the coach and waving good-bye to the villagers.

Anne simply beams with pride that her Joachim was singled out for such accolades by the Tsarina. The village folk also congratulate Joachim. Some jokingly bow to him and say, "Shall we call you 'sir,' now that you have touched the Tsarina's hand?" Still, a handful of people look disdainfully at Joachim and leave, something that does not go unnoticed by Anne. Thus, all is not as well as it might appear. Trouble is fomenting in "paradise," and it will surely surface.

✦

This year, 1787, the council elections begin with a number of men running for office. Joachim presents himself as a candidate. His credentials are good, and his name is listed. Joachim and the Stampe family have excellent reputations in Urbach and have proved to be solid supporters of the community. Joachim speaks with the villagers about his ambitious plan for Urbach, to make it a central town in the region. Not all are as enthusiastic about such progress, while others simply withhold their opinion. One morning, the week before the election, Joachim is up early, as usual. The first rays of sun set a chorus of roosters crowing in the village. He looks out the window and can hardly believe his eyes. KEIN JUDE FÜR SCHULZ (NO JEW FOR MAYOR), reads a crudely hand-painted sign hung on the gate of his property. Joachim freezes. Before Anne gets up, he runs out to remove the sign. He does not want her to see it and be disturbed.

After his breakfast, he runs down to the village square, where the temporary council office is. He withdraws his name from the election list, to the surprise of the electoral officer. Then he visits the rabbi, expressing his fears.

"Jews are not bad people, from the Christian village people's viewpoint." The rabbi speaks slowly and deliberately. "They like what we do, if they can benefit from it. But dare we sit in control of their lives…?" He shrugs his shoulders. "You did the right thing to withdraw your name from the list. If you want to live a peaceful life, just do your work and enjoy life. But let me tell you, my dear boy, do not ever be fooled by their apparent benevolence.

Now that you know that the 'wolves' are in Urbach, do not expose yourself to them unnecessarily. Be careful!"

Joachim thanks the rabbi for his words of wisdom and rushes back home, determined to sweep all those negative thoughts away and enjoy life. Anne is already dressed and has fed the children. She is leaning over the wooden tub, washing their clothes, when Joachim arrives back home. *Oh, what a gorgeous woman*, he muses, as he views her shapely behind. He walks over to her and gives her a big bear hug and a sloppy kiss.

"Ooooh, you naughty boy," she says with much delight. Joachim takes her by the hand, and, giggling like a pair of teenage lovers, they run into the hay shed.

Little Reuben is born on February 28, 1789, before the onset of the now-regular cholera season. The midwife from Enders delivers the baby while Joachim is at the village well, breaking the ice and bringing the bucket of water into the house. He has severe misgivings about putting his son through this ritual. When he does, there is an almighty yell from a pair of very healthy lungs, and Joachim cringes. The boy is then rubbed dry and wrapped in a warm blanket and given to Anne. Of all the children, he seems the most robust at birth.

The election is held successfully and Christian Müller, the teacher, is duly appointed as mayor. Much attention is now given to the security of the growing village, but the overwhelming problem is the distribution of land to the ever-increasing number of settlers choosing this area, as well as the young men who are growing up and starting their own families, who need fields to produce food. This means that either fields are obtained farther and farther away from Urbach and worked into arable land or the existing farms are reduced in size to cater to the new generations and their families. This predicament in itself raises security issues.

Chapter 11
Chameleonic Paradise

"Let the great world spin forever down the ringing grooves of change."
—*Alfred, Lord Tennyson*

THE SAD NEWS OF ESTHER'S DEATH IS VERY HARD FOR JOACHIM TO BEAR. After a short illness, she died from acute Kidney failure. Sergey was at her side when she passed away. But Sergey did not outlive her by very much. He grieved for Esther so deeply that he died peacefully in his sleep two weeks later. Joachim informs Peter and Johanna in Enders on his way to St. Petersburg. Peter and Johanna express their condolences to Joachim. They are genuinely sad to hear of her and Sergey's death. This may be the last time they meet with Joachim.

Peter is amazingly well for his advancing years, still doing some work in his forge. However, most of the heavy work is now done by his twin sons, Gottlieb and Philip, who have built it into a fine business. They have each built their own home on their father's property and are raising their families there. Gottlieb has five children. His eldest son, Robert, is already showing great skill at making jewellery, which he is learning from his *Oma* (grandma). Philip has four daughters and three sons. They all work hard to provide food and clothing for their growing families. Rosanna has also married and lives nearby, in the village Rosenheim. She often visits her adoptive parents, and they see each other in church.

An itinerant pastor comes once a month to the local church. On the other Sundays, the local teacher, takes on the Sunday sermons, since Enders has now established its own school. Much attention is given to the Bible and to preserving the German language and Hessian culture. Since Rosanna's children also attend the school in Enders, any school activity is another opportunity for her and her children to associate with members of the family.

When Joachim arrives in St. Petersburg, the city does not have the same charm for him as it did some thirty years ago, when everything was new and romantic and life was full of promise. The solicitor informs Joachim that everything in the Ivanovs' estate has been willed to him, since Sergey had no children and Joachim is Esther's only son. They have left an amount of 60,000 rubles in their bank account, and the estate is valued at 72,000 rubles. "Unfortunately, Mr. Hahn, the estate will have to be returned to the crown," says the lawyer, in his cold, matter-of-fact way of dealing with such matters. "Jews under the Russian law may not buy or own real estate. However, you may claim some of your mother's belongings, if you wish. The money in the bank account is yours, of course, minus our fees and the tax to the crown. That will leave you with a total amount of"—he scribbles some figures on a piece of paper—"forty-one thousand rubles. Now, you may sign here and we will hand you over the money."

Joachim is disgusted, but he signs it anyway.

"Are there any of your mother's belongings you wish to secure?"

"Yes, sir, I would like to have my mother's violins."

"That is fine. We will accompany you to the Ivanovs' estate."

When Joachim enters the house, he cannot believe his eyes. There is hardly a piece of furniture left. The paintings are gone, as well as the piano. Joachim looks aghast at the lawyer, who simply shrugs his shoulders. He rushes up to his mother's bedroom to search for the violins. They are nowhere to be found, nor is any of his mother's jewellery. Joachim's anger rises in him like a tidal wave. Then he recalls his mother's last words to him while she was in Urbach. He asks the lawyer if he can be left alone in the bedroom for a little while, as it was here that his mother died. The lawyer respectfully steps outside.

When Joachim is sure that the guy is out of earshot, he begins to tap the wall panels. They all make a dull, low-pitched sound. But then he hears the panel with the higher pitch. He quickly looks around to make sure that no one is there. But the panel does not budge, no matter what he tries. He thinks of a strategy. So he begins singing a Jewish dirge, and gradually he lets out cries. Then, as he screams loudly, his large fist smashes into the wood-panelled wall, which falls out under the impact and his rage subsides. Two violin cases are placed neatly behind the panel. Joachim's hand trembles as he pulls out the first one. He opens it and sees his mother's violin wrapped in soft cloth. Great relief comes over Joachim as he closes the case. He then pulls out the second violin case. He opens it, takes a brief peek, and quickly shuts it again. For a second he stands stunned, but gathers his composure. He quickly replaces the panel just before the lawyer walks back into the room.

"I see you have found the violins, Mr. Hahn," the lawyer says, pointing with his head to the two cases under Joachim's arms.

"Yes, thank you, sir. We can go now. The sooner I put this behind me, the better."

The lawyer does not question the contents of the violin cases. He is just happy to have those signed papers in his hot hands.

One week later, Joachim returns to Urbach. Still grieving, he is angry about what they have done to his mother's estate. However, Anne sees the "glass as half full" and helps Joachim determine what they can do with the money: they can do some work on the homestead and help their children, who are growing up. Joachim and Anne decide to divide the money equally among the five children, with 7,000 rubles for each child. They will spend the rest on more horses and cows and on upgrading the stables, as well as on making substantial alterations to the homestead.

Later, after dinner on his first night back from St. Petersburg, Joachim brings out the second violin case and puts it on the table. Anne's jaw drops when she sees all the jewellery and gold coins. There is a little note in the case that says, *I hope you will find this, Joachim! Please keep the papers; they may save your life or the lives of your children someday.* There are the original visa papers that state Esther is "German," the marriage certificate that states that she is "German" and Russian Orthodox by religion, Esther's baptism certificate, and her appointment papers to the orchestra. Anne puts these away safely. Then they look through the jewellery and select which pieces to keep and pass on to their children, and some that may be sold.

Aaron, who has left home, receives his inheritance immediately. He has moved to Enders, where he is apprenticed to a printer. He is now married to a lovely lass from Enders but converted to be a Lutheran in order to marry her. He has one son, Eduard, and a daughter, Maria. Having married into an influential family gives him a start in setting up his own printing business. An opportunity arises for him to acquire a building in Saratov that not only will suit his printing needs but also will provide great business connections. He needs 6,000 rubles to get started. His inheritance is a most welcome present. Joachim and Anne are pleased for Aaron.

However, 1796 is a calamitous year. In addition to Esther's death, a national tragedy occurs on November 6. News reaches Saratov that Her Imperial Majesty Catherine II the Great has died. The settlers wonder how the change in government might affect them. However, they need not worry. The successor to Catherine II is her son Paul I. His relationship with his mother was acrimonious. Hence, when he comes to the throne he reverses many of the harsh decisions his mother made, in particular those that allow the Russian nobility to exploit the lower classes and live decadent lives, something that Joachim experienced firsthand in St. Petersburg a few months ago. The army also comes under Paul I's scrutiny, but he makes some bad decisions that destabilize the military and that lead to his murder on March 23, 1801.

※

Since Aaron has taken to the printing trade, Jacob is left to learn his father's trade. He has a particular flair for this work. When he was in his late twenties, he lived with his brother in Saratov for a year. There he learned the art of casting bronze, which he then used to make rails and handles and ornaments for the better-class coaches he built with his father. Jacob becomes well-known in the district. Working in the field and in his workshop keep him busy, and he makes good money. He may need it, because by the age of forty-one, he already has eight children and his wife, Louise, is expecting again.

※

Louise Schneider is the last of eleven children born to Wilhelm and Ingrid Schneider from the village of Mariental. Wilhelm Schneider is a good man. He worked hard to provide for his family as a caring father and husband. Unfortunately, his wife, Ingrid, was raped and impregnated by a Kirkizer in a raid. Being a good Jewish wife, she found it hard to come to terms with bearing the child of one of these "monsters." "I love this child because God wants it to live, but I hate this child because it is a Kirkizer's child," Ingrid said repeatedly as the emotional conflict in her kept growing along with the child. Wilhelm assured her of his love over and over again. Ingrid, however, slipped into a deep depression shortly after Louise's birth. She never recovered from it, and when Louise was just three years old, Ingrid hanged herself in the family stables on the fourth anniversary of the raid. Wilhelm raised the family on his own with the help of his two eldest daughters. He loves Louise as much as he does his other ten children.

For Louise, however, her Mongolian facial features are the cause of much discrimination against her from the villagers. This may well be based on jealousy. "God has compensated Louise," says Wilhelm, "by giving her rare beauty." That beauty is not just on her face but also on the inside. Not that she is the only Kirkizer child in the village; however, she is also a full-fledged Jewess, by virtue of her mother. She has grown to be a fine woman with a very big heart, a wonderful wife to Jacob, and a happy, contented mother to their children. Joachim and Anne are enjoying their roles as grandparents to their little ones, and now another is on the way.

Johannes is born in March 1809 and is duly dipped in ice water. He is not as tall as the other children. He has broad shoulders like his grandfather Joachim but the stocky build of a Kirkizer. But the apparent serenity in the village is the calm before the storm. Turbulent times are ahead for Jacob and all the villagers.

❂

Jacob sits on the bed next to his dying father, holding his hand. Louise and the children stand respectfully at the end of the bed. Anne sits on the other side of the bed, holding Joachim's other hand. It is all the result of a terrible accident. A horse was spooked when a dog attacked a goose, which promptly flew up in front of the horse. Joachim was standing behind the horse, and it kicked Joachim in the chest. The injury led to an infection in Joachim's lungs. The doctor is attending to patients in Mariental, and messengers have gone to fetch him, but it seems all too late. When he finally arrives, he informs Anne and Jacob that there is nothing he can do for Joachim.

Anne Catherine, Karl, and Reuben also stand at the end of the bed. Anne Catherine is twenty-five years old and has not yet married. Karl is twenty-three, Reuben twenty-one and both still live at home. They are all good workers and help to keep the farm and the business going.

Is Aaron coming?" Joachim asks with a raspy voice.

"He will be here soon," Anne assures him. In his will, Joachim has entrusted all his business to Jacob and charged him with looking after his mother. Joachim reminds him of this part of the will. "There is something special I want you to care for; it is your grandmother's violin. Please treasure it."

Aaron never makes it to say good-bye to his father. Instead, a letter arrives after the funeral explaining his problem. He had to work on a very important printing job with his father-in-law. It would have meant a great financial loss for them. After Anne and Jacob read the letter, Jacob throws it into the burning hearth. *I don't like Aaron's attitude. He seems to be taking the Protestant line of his wife's family,* Jacob ponders. *I wonder if we will hear from him again.* And wonder he might. With the reign of Tsar Alexander I, instability returns to Russia because of his on-and-off friendship with Napoleon, which leads to the French invasion of Russia in 1812. The whole campaign takes its toll on Russia, and the settlers along the Volga River feel the impact of the war.

At forty-eight years of age, Aaron, who is now a nominal Christian, is drafted into the armed conflict with the French. Aaron's boys work with their grandfather in the printing business to keep it going while their father is transported to the vicinity of Moscow. The Russian army forms a plan to follow the rear of the French, to prevent them from escaping. The climax of the war comes when Napoleon lays siege against Moscow but is soundly defeated, ending the French connection with Russia forever. When the French retreat from the battle of Moscow, Aaron's army division confronts the French in an ambush. While the Russians inflict great losses on the retreating French, it is not without cost to the Russians.

Aaron's father-in-law informs Anne of her stepson's death. Jacob feels a tinge of regret that he burned Aaron's last letter. Aaron is buried in Enders, with both families in attendance. Aaron's widow and her children move to Saratov permanently.

Living Among Wolves

There is a large German population in that city that will ensure the survival of the German language. However, it will also provide better educational opportunities for Aaron's children, as well as keeping the printing business going. Anne takes the deaths of her husband and her stepson, so close to each other, badly. She dies in May 1820 of pneumonia and is buried next to Joachim and Elisabeth.

※

Farming is becoming a problem for the Volga Germans. Not only are the allotments becoming smaller as they are divided between the children and their families, but the yields are becoming lesser because the soil is exhausted from more intense farming. Many are moving away to areas where there are opportunities to make a good life for their families. Most of Jacob's children move to the Ukraine, the Crimea, or the Caucasus regions, where there are some German villages. Louise finds this difficult to deal with. She is a dedicated mother who misses her offspring. Her only consolation is that Johannes decides to remain closer to home and carry on his father's coach-building business. He is spending more and more time in nearby Mariental, where a Jewish girl named Fridericke Rubinstein lives. When he marries her, Louise is comforted. "At least there will be some grandchildren to love," she says. And a grandmother she does become, with fifteen grandchildren from Johannes alone. However, ominous signs appear on the political horizon that once again threatens to destabilize Jewish life in the region.

※

After Tsar Alexander I dies, Nicholas I succeeds him on the imperial throne. One of his first acts as the new emperor is to abolish local autonomy. This has a huge impact on the hitherto-self-governed villages. The Jewish communities in particular are a target of Nicholas I, who removes all *qahals* (self-governance of Jewish communities). *The Cantonist Decrees,* as they become known, force the conscription of Jewish boys between the ages of twelve and eighteen into the Russian army for a period of twenty-five years. During their time in the army, every effort is made to Christianize the boys. This pressure on them causes many deaths by suicide, or they simply do not survive the harsh treatment meted out to them. Jewish mothers are so desperate to save their boys from this fate that they disfigure them, making them unsuitable for military service. Some cut off their son's index finger so he cannot use the trigger on a rifle.

A sadistic streak is added to this tragedy, in that the Jewish community leaders have to select the boys who will go into the army. In fact, they have to meet a certain quota of boys. The heartache is too much for some to bear, and they accept the fate of execution for failure to select the boys. In Urbach, the Jewish rabbi is deported to Siberia for uttering dissent, saying in public, "The emperor has gone to bed with the church!" This sends a strong signal to the rest of the Jews there to be very careful. On the other hand, it emboldens those with radical views to take liberties with the Jews and their properties.

Nicholas I also introduces new conservative principles of loyalty to the emperor and the Russian Orthodox Church, applicable to *all* people living in Russia. This causes a major outcry by the Lutheran communities, as well as the Catholic villages and the Mennonites. With that, Tsar Nicholas I begins a campaign of repression of thought by introducing severe censorship laws. The newspapers in Russia are now carefully monitored.

Eduard Hahn, son of Aaron Hahn, is a major player in establishing the first newspaper in Saratov in 1835 for the German readers. It is called the *Saratov Volkszeitung (Saratov Newspaper for German Folk).* The newspaper comes immediately under severe scrutiny by the Tsar, especially since it is printed in German; the Tsar wants to ensure not only that the emperor's new ideals are well reported on and that his vanity is fed with many accolades, but that the newspaper subtly encourages his anti-Semitic sentiments.

For Eduard, this is very hard, for he knows that his cousins, who have not converted to Christianity like his father, will suffer as a consequence. "This is yet another reversal of the Catherine II manifesto that guaranteed freedom of worship," he complains to his co-editor. The whole idea is distasteful to him, as it also affects his Lutheran relatives. But neutrality is not an option under Tsar Nicholas I. Despite all of this, new growth in the *Wolgagebiet* (Volga region) continues.

The rapid increase of new arrivals from Germany and the astounding numbers of children born in this region causes the founding of new villages everywhere. From Krasny Kut, on the north side of the Jeruslan River develop the villages of Hoffental and Rosental. On the southern side spring up Schöntal, Schönfeld, and Schöndorf. Together they present a formidable cluster of villages. David, the son of Johannes Hahn, sees the opportunity to establish himself in the village of Rosental, recently founded in 1855, just after the death of Tsar Nicholas I. Their nearness to Krasny Kut, a major centre of business, gives these villages a distinct advantage for conducting business and selling agricultural produce.

With such population growth in the *Wolgagebiet*, the raids by the Kirkizers almost disappear, much to the relief of all villagers. This may also be due in part to the ever-increasing friendly relations developing between the German and the Russian villages. As the Russian language becomes a second language to the younger generations, their social interactions increase. In the winter, it is not uncommon for Russian visitors to arrive in the evenings at a familiar German home.

Amelia, David's wife, opens the door one late afternoon. In the snowdrift to the front entrance stands Igor, from the nearby Russian village of Yagodnaya, in his brown fur coat and hat. The falling snow covers his shoulders and sleeves. Igor is well known to David, as he sometimes comes to have some repairs done to his wagon and, of course, to chat. Igor walks into the very warm house, after shaking the snow off his fur coat. He then throws it onto the floor and falls upon it. Thereafter, the niceties of a home visit begin, as he greets the family with a hearty "good evening." David also lays his bearskin on the floor and makes himself comfortable, as does David's neighbor Jacob. Amelia knows the routine and gets a dish in which she warms some vodka. She hands each of the men a cup after placing the dish of vodka in front of them. The potbellied stove is glowing red-hot. Each man dips his cup in the vodka, and then the chatting begins. Tonight, however, the conversation has a sombre tone.

Igor starts: "What do you think, David —now that Tsar Nicholas I is dead, will Russia be a better place for us all under Tsar Alexander II?"

"No, Igor, I don't believe it will. And you want to know why? Well, for one thing, militarily Russia is exhausted after losing the Crimean War. We, the farmers, will have to carry the financial burden to revitalize an already corrupt government. The government needs money. Why do you think the Tsar sold Alaska to the Americans?"

"That useless piece of land?" Jacob snarls. "It was of no use to Russia, and did we get even one ruble or a bottle of vodka?"

"Corruption is everywhere, Jacob," David continues. "Have you tried lately to deal with the authorities in Samara, Saratov, or Novouzensk? You must come with an open wallet, my friend, if you want their ear."

"Alexander II is not popular," says Igor. "Some of the more powerful and influential families have already attempted to assassinate him for his reforms. Especially for the emancipation of the serfs! They are losing their cheap labor!"

Jacob raises an interesting point: "What about the good reforms he made? Surely the railway systems that Nicholas I started and that Alexander II has now greatly expanded must benefit us all here in the *Wolgagebiet*. The Rayazan–Ural Railway to Saratov is a great idea.

Krasny Kut will also be part of this railway system. That will save a lot of time and money to transport our goods to major centres."

"But, Jacob," David interrupts, "railways can also bring a lot of trouble and greater control by the government."

As they chat late into the night, the vodka and the heat take their toll and the men fall asleep on their bearskins. Amelia brings out some blankets, puts them over the snoring bodies, and returns to her bed. The men's foreboding thoughts are not unwarranted.

Anxiety turns into panic when the Tsar officially rescinds *all* the conditions set out in Catherine II's manifesto. All foreign males must now accept military service. Also, taxation will be increased. All village and local government is to be abolished. Russian will be taught in the schools. Russian army personnel will be stationed in each village and take control. There will be a single nationality in Russia and a single religion—Russian Orthodox.

Mennonites and many others who see the writing on the wall immediately begin to sell whatever they can and book their passage out of Russia to America and Canada. For them it is impossible to stay in Russia, since they object to military service. They know that any resistance will be met with the full Russian force of either execution, deportation to Siberia, or, at best, expulsion. So the Mennonites, by and large, leave on their own terms, as do many others. The economic and moral impact on the Volga settlements is felt immediately.

❖

Back in Enders, the Hardt clan is spreading. Most of them have converted to the Lutheran faith, the hitherto-dominant religion in Enders. A number are settling in Saratov, where Philip was born. Philip Hardt marries Maria Richter from Urbach. He then decides to settle in her village to follow in his great-grandfather's footsteps as a great organizer and a skilled mason. In Urbach he has the opportunity to design and build stone buildings, such as the village council building and the Lutheran church. He and Maria have twenty-one children. Not all survive, due to the continuing cholera plague each year. The eldest son, Konrad Philip, is also a stonemason and helps with his father's construction work. Alexander concerns himself with the family farm, but in his leisure time, mostly in winter, he reads a lot. He often travels to Saratov to spend time in the library. When he returns, he has much to tell his siblings, who sit spellbound by his stories.

He and his twin sister, Pauline, were born on March 31, 1886, and thus escaped the "baptism" in icy water. She is especially fascinated by what Alex has to say about faraway places and strange people. His tales really fire Pauline's imagination. And a good imagination she has, particularly anything relating to the mysterious or gruesome. Even from a young age, she entertained her friends in the village with outrageous stories. Yet she has a penchant for remembering details and historical events as if they were chiselled on stone tablets. Nothing that happens in her family or the village is lost in her mind.

◊

Tsar Alexander II is particularly disliked by the growing revolutionaries in Russia. So it comes as a little surprise when he is assassinated by revolutionaries in St. Petersburg on March 13, 1881, when a bomb was thrown at him. His son Alexander III succeeds him. Following Tsar Alexander III's edicts, the government enforces many of the new laws of his father, Alexander II, on a much greater scale. However, any liberation his father proclaimed is quickly reversed to stamp his authority on his oppressive reign, as evidenced by his insistence on a singular religion and singular language in Russia. Pauline, who is not academically inclined, has a difficult time learning Russian in school and finds it unbearable not to speak in German there; to tell her stories in Russian is too hard. The presence of Russian soldiers in the village, and at times in the classroom, makes all feel uncomfortable. Since local German government is abolished, villagers now have to present all matters to the Russians to decide on and to receive orders from them. However, as is the German nature, they make the best of the situation and, through the liberal sharing of vodka, the villagers generally get on just fine with the Russians. Alex masters the Russian language very well and teaches his siblings some of the basics, much to the annoyance of his mother, Maria.

May 1882 is etched in the minds of all the Jews in Russia. Because of what are known as the *May Laws,* Jews are banned from inhabiting rural areas and have severe restrictions placed on the kinds of occupations they may pursue. David is teaching his son Friedrich the trades of coach building and coopering—definite no-nos under the new law. Naturally, he is very concerned on that point and about the fact that he is the only Jew living in Rosental, although so far, no one knows (or so he thinks). He takes desperate measures, meticulously destroying any papers relating to his Jewish heritage, including his birth and marriage certificates. He travels to Novouzensk, where he previously registered the birth of his son Friedrich in 1869. With an open wallet, he sees a Russian official and explains that all his papers were destroyed in a fire. (In saying this, he does not lie.)

The registrar looks David up and down. David is hoping that he will not ask him to drop his pants for a physical examination to check if he is circumcised. He is relieved when the registrar asks him, "Do you have any evidence of your ancestry?"

David produces his great-great-grandmother Esther's papers, which his great-grandfather Joachim passed down in the family. The papers state that his ancestry is German and his religion is Russian Orthodox. That satisfies the registrar, and with the right sort of "incentive," he issues new documentation based on David's sworn statement. Hence, no references to his being Jewish are now on paper. Flushed with victory, David returns to Rosental, having averted yet another crisis—for the moment.

Given the harsh new Russian measures, the villagers are struggling to survive on their trades and farm produce. Yet for the moment, life in Rosental and the rest of the villages goes on, uneventful but watchful. However, death and destruction on a major scale are lurking around the corner, and the enemy is a totally new one.

❖

The winter of 1890–91 begins in an unusual manner. The snow, which normally starts in October, does not arrive. This is a bad omen for the farmers in the *Wolgagebiet*. Without the snow cover, the winter crops they have sown die in the extreme frosts. Still, they are optimistic that some seeds will grow in the spring. This last hope is dashed when extreme flooding of the Volga covers vast regions of the arable land and then freezes over into enormous sheets of ice. The Jeruslan River also floods and life in Rosental comes to a standstill. Not knowing the extent and severity of the disaster, David, along with everyone else in Rosental, is concerned that there will be not enough fodder for the horses and the rest of the domestic animals, since the floods also destroy that and reserves are running low. Rationing becomes the order of the day.

Then spring comes with uncommonly strong winds that erode topsoil and any hope of planting seeds. Finally, adding insult to injury, the summer heat starts in April, much earlier than usual, and produces a very long and dry spell that is hitherto unknown.

The result is a huge famine that grips the region, starting along the Volga, and then moving east to the Urals and south to the Crimea. The normally cholera-resilient people, who have lived on severe rationing for over a year, have no immunity to deal with the extreme plague that follows the next spring. As a result, some five hundred thousand people die from the famine and the cholera. Some villages are close to being obliterated.

Among the desperate measures to survive is the option to leave the country or to move to other parts of the country. The steady stream of wagons rolling toward Saratov is a pitiful sight. For the villagers, life in the *Wolgagebiet* is all they have known, worked for, and loved. The options are closed for many, and tearfully they leave all behind. They cannot sell the land and the buildings on it, for they never owned the land; they were just "guests" of the imperial court. From the Hardt family in Urbach, Konrad Philip, Pauline's brother, uproots his family and moves to the northern Caucasus city of Gnadenburg in the hope that the famine has not reached that far. David Hahn's brother, Joachim, named after his great-grandfather, moves all the way to the eastern city of Omsk, some 1,300 kilometres away. Families are torn apart on an unprecedented scale, setting off yet another diaspora, particularly in the Jewish communities.

Criticism of the Tsar's handling of this disaster is heard everywhere. The *Saratov Volkszeitung* carries an article by Leo Tolstoy, who is heavily involved in famine relief, blaming the Tsar and the Russian Orthodox Church for this debacle. The result is that the Russian court is pushed into action to raise money for the victims of the famine. The Tsar reinstates local village councils, except Jewish councils, to assist with the famine-relief work. However, it is too little, too late. Many people are relieved when news reaches Saratov that Alexander III has died of renal failure. Now the "wolves" are becoming really savage, and God help the Jews!

Chapter 12
In the Shadows of Pogroms

"The wolf don't count the sheep." —Virgil

TSAR NICHOLAS II accedes to the throne on March 2, 1894. The outcry over the Tsar's corruption is great. Seeds of discontent are everywhere, and the military savagely puts down rebellions. Political opponents are instantly dealt with through executions. The people's focus on the Russian throne becomes too intense, and the Tsar must take measures to turn the spotlight away from him. As the twentieth century begins, the Russian secret police starts to circulate an anti-Semitic document called "The Protocol of the Elders of Zion." This spurious document claims to be the minutes of a meeting of Jewish world leaders that outlines a plot to gain world control in the new century. Hence, it makes it appear that the problems the Russian crown faces are caused not by the greed of the nobility but by an age-old scapegoat—the Jews.

◈

In Rosental, in the summer of 1897, Friedrich, despite his father's misgivings, marries a Jewish girl, Rosanna Meier, from the village of Schöndorf, situated just across the Jeruslan River. There are some malcontents who want to disrupt the wedding, but a formidable group of friends and family quickly send them on their way. A few months later, Rosanna becomes pregnant. Her pregnancy does not go well, and she is confined to bed for much of the time. Rosanna is a frail girl at the best of times, and her pregnancy drains her energy. The midwife tells Friedrich that she is a little concerned for Rosanna's well-being. However, in the month before the birth, she picks up a little and feels confident about the delivery. She goes into labor late on June 30, and the going is hard. The midwife stays with her day and night. Finally, she gives birth to a little girl, but Rosanna never gets to see her or hold her in her arms. The labor is too much for her, and she dies. Friedrich takes the child and breaks down in sobs. The joy of the new child and the loss of his beautiful wife are emotions too contradictory to remain close to each other. He hands the child to the midwife and runs out into the street, where he drops to his knees and lets out a roar that comes from the deepest part of his soul. Neighbors rush over to comfort him.

Rosanna's family, after hearing the news, comes quickly to be with Friedrich and to cry with him. "How will you take care of Elisabeth, Friedrich?" Rosanna's mother asks. "Do you want us to take her with us until you can cope again?"

Friedrich is once again torn between the child whom he so loves, and who is a reminder of her mother, and knowing that it would be best for Elisabeth to be taken care of for a while. So he agrees.

"You must come often, Friedrich, to see her, and we shall also bring her over to you from time to time." The Meier family stays for a few days to help Friedrich. David, Friedrich's father, also helps out with farm work, since it is right at the beginning of the harvest. Then, stating all their assurances again that it is in the best interest of all that Elisabeth will be taken care of by the Meier family, they leave with little Elisabeth.

Friedrich is concerned when he hears of some pogroms that are starting to target Jewish communities. *Pogrom* is a Russian word meaning "devastation." Initially, these pogroms are few and intermittent. Although, at first, only two Jews are killed, the effect of these disturbances is dramatic. Jewish emigration now gathers momentum. In no time, the diaspora is in full swing. Most emigrate to America. Friedrich's Jewish background is not well known, if at all. Still, he fears for the safety of the Meier family and his own. *Complacency is the worst position to take*, Friedrich reminds himself. He visits the Meiers often and stays a day or two to spend time with his rapidly growing daughter. By now she is six years old. Friedrich hopes that soon he will be able to take Elisabeth back to Rosenthal but he is not quite ready for that yet.

In 1903, the pogroms take on an even uglier face. Over the next three years, two thousand Jews will die and countless more will be wounded. The pogroms in Odessa are by far the worst. There, 2,500 Jews lose their lives. A mass exodus ensues. The Jews are leaving in droves, destabilizing the region even more—first the Mennonites left; now the Jews. The hitherto-close-knit fabric of the villages now has its social and commercial heart torn apart. To say that uncertainty rules the lives of the villagers is a terrible understatement.

David, feeling somewhat safe, visits Urbach from time to time and catches up with the Hardt family. Alex is drafted into the army and sent to Japan to fight the Russo-Japanese War. Pauline, who is close to her twin brother, frets for him. David, who is becoming quite concerned about Friedrich's being on his own for so long, speaks with Pauline's parents about how they might feel about arranging a marriage between Pauline and Friedrich. They seem to be very pleased, knowing that the Hardts and the Hahns have a long connection.

Friedrich is a little annoyed at his father's action but thinks about the possibility of marrying again. So, unbeknownst to David, he visits Urbach under some lousy pretense. And while he is there, he nonchalantly calls on the Hardts "just to say hello." Suddenly, there stands Pauline. He has not seen her since she was a girl of about eight. He is a little gob-smacked.

"Friedrich, how good to see you," she says, and gives him a hug that sends all sorts of messages through his confused body. "Please come in and stay for dinner and spend the night here. It is much too cold and dangerous to travel back to Rosental in this awful weather."

Friedrich accepts graciously. Over dinner, he cannot keep his eyes off Pauline. Later, Pauline's parents, Philip and Maria, sit and talk with Friedrich over a cup of heart-warming vodka. Pauline has already gone to bed. When Friedrich speaks of his wife's death and his little girl, Elisabeth, the Hardts have tears in their eyes, as does Friedrich. "Still, Elisabeth is taken good care of by her grandparents until I can manage to have her home again."

"Now, Fried," asks Philip, "you did not come here accidentally, did you?"

Friedrich is a little shocked by this leading question. But, being a sort of straight shooter himself, he admits that he is impressed with Pauline. "If you are thinking of asking Pauline to marry you, please be assured that you have our blessing, Fried. It will be a wonderful thing to bring our two families close together, as they were once before."

After breakfast the next morning, Pauline's parents and nine siblings disappear, leaving Friedrich and Pauline alone. Friedrich proposes marriage to Pauline, who is delighted to accept his offer.

"I wish my brother Alex was here on our wedding day," Pauline whispers to Friedrich. "I miss him so much. He is my best friend." Friedrich hugs his bride tightly. He feels for Pauline and has difficulty restraining his tears. In his pocket is a letter from the Japanese front, though Pauline is not aware of it. Her father gave it to Friedrich the day before the wedding. "Please, Fried, break the news to her gently," Philip begged. The letter reads: *Mr. Philip Hardt, the Russian army command regrets to inform you that your son Alexander Hardt was mortally wounded in combat. He served his country with dignity and honor.*

In the Shadows of Pogroms

By the following year, Japan has defeated the Russians. Friedrich then breaks the news to Pauline, which devastates her. Some days later, the Meier family arrives with Elisabeth so that she can stay with her father and her new mother, Pauline. This happens just in time, for a few weeks later, the Meier family is unceremoniously forced out of Schöndorf. They have no time to say good-bye to their granddaughter Elisabeth.

✧

Late one afternoon, a group of Tsarist thugs combs the Schöndorf and rounds up all the Jews. They herd the Jews onto a couple of wagons by beating them with heavy clubs that break bones and cause deep lacerations. They then tie their hands to the wagons like handcuffed prisoners. They show no respect even for old men and women. The hatred oozes out of their eyes and mouths.

A little way out of the village, they stop at two heaps of timber and straw and drive the wagons between them. After releasing the horses, they set the wood and straw on fire while watching the men, women, and children burn to death. Their screams of agony and pleas for mercy are met with scorn and laughter. The brutality of this action is to serve notice to any Jews in the region to leave or face the consequences. Jews everywhere run in panic to get out of Russia as the news is quickly passed around.

Over the river in Rosental, a child frets for her grandparents. "Why are Oma and Opa Meier not coming to see me anymore?" asks Elisabeth.

Pauline just hugs Elisabeth and kisses her gently. "One day you will see them again," she says. With that, she instantly makes up the most wonderful story of how and when and where they will meet again for a most joyful reunion. "In a land called Prussia, where there is plenty of food and the people live peacefully with one another, there is a benign ruler called the Kaiser who visits all his subjects to make sure they are happy. Everyone has a home and land, and no one makes any trouble. Then one day, while you sit by one of the thousand lakes in a place called Masuria, Oma and Opa Meier will come sailing by in their boat to pick you up and take you across the lake to where they have the most beautiful home, with servants and lots and lots of animals to play with. Your papa and I love that place so much that we will build our home next to Oma and Opa Meier, and then we will never have to be away from each other again."

Elisabeth falls asleep blissfully in Pauline's arms. *You poor, innocent child*, Pauline thinks. *If only we knew what awaits us.* They do not have the heart to tell her what really happened to Oma and Opa Meier.

Rather than run in panic, Friedrich and his father, David, take a calculated risk. They decide to remain in Russia for the time being, believing that their Jewish identity is covered.

Aside from the bloody pogroms sanctioned by the Tsar, the year 1905 earns him the dubious title Bloody Nicholas, for a very specific incident. On January 22, a peaceful demonstration by the working class marches to the Winter Palace in St. Petersburg to present a petition to Tsar Nicholas II. The Tsar orders his army to confront the demonstrators. Then he gives the order to kill. The massacre is enormous. The Russian people are in disbelief that such brutal force should be used on unarmed people. This spells the beginning of the end for normal life in Russia for all, including the Tsar. The Russian people are not prepared to let this act go without dire consequences. The Russian Revolution is born. Vengeance and hatred know no bounds. In this climate of anger, it is easy to inflame the population with distorted information.

✦

Amid this turmoil and the continued harassment of any Jews remaining in Russia, Salomon is born on January 22, 1906. He, too, has to undergo the "baptism" in icy water. For Friedrich, providing for his family means hard work on the farm and in his workshop. Given the mass exodus of people, the demand for wagons, coaches, and wooden kegs is greatly diminishing. Extra land to cultivate is available, but the presence of Russian soldiers will not allow anyone to cultivate unused land. Friedrich tries hard to keep good relations with the Russians, knowing that they are under command by the Tsar to enforce his ideals. So he tries not to take it personally. Occasionally the Russians will pay the Hahns a visit in winter and spend the night there over a tub of vodka that Pauline has ready. In these situations, the Hahn family develops a great fondness for the Russian people. Young Salomon takes in everything he sees and hears and picks up the Russian language with great ease. Eventually, their good relations with the Russians prove to be a lifeline for the Hahn family. Even during the harvest times, some soldiers come and give Friedrich a hand to bring in the loads.

Salomon's grandfather David is preoccupied these days with getting his home and affairs in order. He owns a sizable number of horses, which he breeds and sells. Lately he seems distant and tight-lipped much to Friedrich's consternation. It thus comes as a surprise when, early in the winter of 1912, among the turmoil in Russia, David visits Friedrich and tells him about his intended visit to his brother Joachim in Omsk. Even more surprised is Salomon when his grandfather invites him to go with him. "It is such a long way, Friedrich, and God knows I can do with some bright company like Salomon," David pleads.

"How are you going to do that? With wolves everywhere, you must face some great dangers." Friedrich is quite concerned.

David pulls out a piece of paper with some diagrams indicating the way he wants to go to Omsk. "First we will go by horse and sled to Novousensk. Don't worry, Fried, there are four sleds coming with us to Novousensk. We all have rifles, so the wolves should not be a problem. Salomon and I will get on the Rayazan–Ural train to Uralsk, then Orenburg, and then Omsk. We will stay with my brother for a month, and then we will make our way back. We will pick up the horse and sled in Novousensk and see if we can have some people accompany us back to Krasny Kut. From there we will be all right by ourselves."

As David concludes his outline of the trip, Salomon looks expectantly at his father. When is father gives his permission, Salomon is not sure whom to hug first. But Opa David gets the biggest embrace. What an adventure for Salomon!

◊

As the sun is setting, an hour or so out of Novousensk, a pack of wolves spots the caravan of sleds. David asks one of the other people on the sled to take over the reins of his sled while he rides on the back of it. Another sled then lines up next to his with the same formation: two in the lead and two at the rear. As the pack appears out of the woods, David cautions the group not to get trigger-happy. "At this distance, you are likely to miss, and a bullet whistling past their ears will not deter them. Let them come a bit closer, for I want to see how the pack hunts and who the alpha dog is. Then, when we have him identified at a closer range, we shall fire."

The horses pick up the scent of the wolves and are becoming increasingly nervous. It is up to the leading sleds to keep the pace going. The other two will follow closely. Salomon is very excited and a little scared, having heard his mother's gruesome "wolf stories."

Suddenly the lead driver shouts, "Wolves to your left!" Another pack has picked up the scent of the horses and is spreading out for their attack. Now Salomon crouches down. He is very scared. David takes control. He gives orders to a man on the sled to his left to single out the leader of that pack. "I have got mine selected," he shouts. David is a good shot. A single shot fells the alpha dog.

The rest of the pack stop and surround their dead leader. Then Salomon raises his head. He can hardly believe his eyes as the pack now turn on the dead wolf and start ripping him to pieces. The rider on the left is becoming nervous as the pack takes on a different pattern of attack. David jumps onto his sled and instructs the friend to single out the one on the far left of the pack. He seems to orchestrate the attack. David then takes aim at the one in the middle and fells the dog. The leader, on the left, stops for a second as if his plan has been disrupted.

"Fire!" David shouts to his mate, who does so but misses. By then, David has his rifle reloaded. This dog is very sure of himself. He runs for a little bit, and then stops as if suddenly another plan has emerged in his head. He and two other wolves circle farther ahead and now approach the leading horses from the front. "Turn sharp left." David commands. As the horses do so, the two men get a better sight of the wolves. "Take the one on the left, and don't miss again if you don't want to be his dinner." Then two shots ring out and two wolves fall. The rest of the pack runs back into the forest. Their dinner now lies in the snow.

On the edge of the forest a Russian brown bear comes out. He is curious about what is going on but is very cautious. Raising himself erect, he surveys the traveling sleds but remains at a safe distance, well aware that a good many of his friends have ended up as fur coats for the villagers. The four sleds now make haste to get to Novousensk before dark.

Novousensk is a novelty for Salomon. The next morning, he looks around the large buildings with wonderment in his eyes. But nothing astounds him more than the sight of a locomotive and its train at the station. The steam blowing from beneath the locomotive makes Salomon imagine that this is what one of the dragons from Pauline's stories must be like.

They secure the horses with an innkeeper and pay for their care for the month they will be away. David also leaves his rifles with the innkeeper. They say good-bye to the other three sled drivers and their companions and head off to the train. Beside provisions for the trip, David purchases, in Novousensk, some special treats for Salomon on the trip to Omsk. Now the two are onboard the train as it rocks out of the station. "I hope that I will always be able to recall this wonderful feeling of being on the train with you, Opa David." As the train moves along, Salomon asks, "Were you scared when the wolves attacked, Opa David?"

"Scared? No. Careful? Yes." Then David relates an incident of one summer night when he was camping out in the fields during the harvest. "I was sound asleep, Salomon, when I heard the horse outside my tent becoming restless. When I peeked out of the tent, a lone wolf was coming menacingly close to the horse. I did not wake the other men; I crept out very quietly and went around the back of the tent. The wolf had its back toward me, and the breeze was blowing the other way, so he—I mean, she—did not pick up my scent. I have never seen a wolf so intent on its victim. I got a good look at this miserable creature. It must have been an older female that was cast out of the flock and now had to hunt by herself. The wolf was about to leap up to the horse's neck, when I fell onto it and began to strangle it with my bare hands." He shows Salomon his huge hands. "I believe my great-great-great-grandfather Itzhak had big hands like these. When I strangled the wolf, the squealing noise she made woke up the other men, who looked in amazement at the dead wolf. I guess since that day, I have lost my fear of them."

Salomon sits with his mouth wide open and his eyes fixed on his grandfather's hands. Then he says, "I feel so lucky to have you as my grandfather—I feel safe with you."

※

Omsk, the last city of European Russia, greets them at 5:00 a.m. with incredibly freezing temperatures. Behind Omsk lies the vast region of Siberia. It is a name that has already become notorious for its harsh climate and synonymous with deporting dissidents of the Tsars. Joachim is there to greet them. David and Joachim embrace each other and burst into tears, a side of his grandfather Salomon has not seen. David then introduces Salomon to Joachim. Salomon cannot get over it how much these two men look alike.

Just then, there is another little boy standing behind Joachim. "Oh, Salomon, this is my grandson Peter."

The two boys look shyly at each other, but very soon they are good friends, with their arms around each other, while the men load the luggage onto the coach. "Not as good as the coaches our father built, but they serve their purpose," Joachim comments.

After a hearty breakfast, the two men go and talk while Joachim's daughters and their mother entertain the two boys. David says, "Joachim, I must tell you that my life is coming to its end. I feel tired and find it hard to keep up with the farm and all the work. I wanted to see you one more time to reminisce and to think about all the great times we had as boys. But there is one special reason why I am here. Your eldest daughter, Marlene, has strong musical talents—so you told me in a letter. Have you been able to help her develop this gift?"

"David, as much as I want to, this is very costly, something we cannot afford."

"Then let me help you," says David. He leaves the room and comes back with a large package. "This, Joachim, is the violin belonging to our great-great-grandmother Esther, who was the concertmaster of the St. Petersburg orchestra. Our grandfather Jacob gave it to me to take care of. I have had it all these years, doing nothing, so I want to give it to Marlene. It is a very fine instrument, I believe from what someone said, that would be very costly to buy. It is hers to keep."

"But, David..."

"No, Joachim." David raises his index finger in dissent. "No buts. This is hers, and I know what is next on your mind. *How can I pay for tuition?* Right? Well, you need not worry. I have sold a lot of my animals for a decent sum of money. Friedrich received some of it, and the rest is for Marlene's tuition."

When they present Marlene with this incredible gift and tell her the story behind it, she is totally overwhelmed and cries. There is a fine orchestra in Omsk, and David and Marlene go to search for it. When they locate it, they speak with the orchestra's administrators about finding a suitable tutor. The administrator asks them to take a seat while he goes away. He returns with a smartly dressed lady whom he introduces as Olga Pietrova, a member of the orchestra. After hearing why they came, she looks at Marlene's fingers and checks her posture. "Show me your violin, dear," she asks in a lovely, motherly tone. When she unpacks it, Olga Pietrova looks into the *f*-holes of the violin, reads the distinctive makings inside, and almost drops it. "Do you know what you hold in your hand, girl?"

"No," answers Marlene, looking a bit perplexed.

"You have in your hand the most famous and most precious of violins. It is a Stradivarius! A genuine Stradivarius! In the world of violins, this is the Holy Grail. I have not seen one for decades, let alone held one in my hand. Do you mind if I call some of my colleagues to have a look at it?"

"No, not at all, please do," Marlene stumbles.

Pietrova disappears for a few minutes and emerges with practically the entire Violin section of the orchestra, all of whom want to have a look at this violin.

While the violinists "ooh" and "aah" over the violin and play it, David says to Miss Pietrova, "What about violin lessons for Marlene?"

"What a question, Mr. Hahn. Of course—I will teach her myself. I will make her a great violinist—I promise. I have an hour to spare, Mr. Hahn; may I have this time with Marlene to test out her aptitude and give her the first lesson?"

"Absolutely, Miss…"

"Please, you may call me Olga."

"Then I will amuse myself in your wonderful city of Omsk for an hour or so."

Omsk is very, very cold this winter. Temperatures are consistently around negative forty degrees Celsius. In such bleak conditions, the city does not show a friendly face. While walking along the banks of the river Irtish, he enquires from passersby about some of the notable features of the city. Among other things they point out the remains of the stone fortress that was built around 1760, which replaced the old wooden fortress built in 1716 at the founding of the city. After having satisfied his curiosity about the city, David hurries back to the Omsk Theatre to collect Marlene. On the way back to Marlene's house, she cannot stop speaking of the joy she experienced with Miss Pietrova, and how she played her Stradivarius and made it sing! Spontaneously she leans over and kisses her uncle David. "Thank you for what you have done for me today. I will be eternally grateful to you."

"Marlene, a few weeks ago I had the most vivid dream. I know it was just a dream. But I saw in the dream your great-great-great-grandmother Esther. She was holding the violin in her hand and gave it to me. Then she said, 'Take good care of it David. One day you will find the one to whom it will truly belong.' It seems to me, Marlene, that you have inherited the talents of your great-great-great-grandmother Esther. It is only right that her violin is properly reunited with her talent that is in you. I now feel that I have done my duty to our ancestress. I shall rest in peace. Also"—he reaches deep into his thick coat pocket—"here is the money for your tuition for the next four years. Please take it and use it wisely, like I know you will." Marlene is so overjoyed that she just sobs and hugs her uncle.

❖

Salomon arrives back in Rosenthal with his grandfather, exhausted from the trip but thoroughly exhilarated from the great adventure. He learned such a lot about people and life. He tells his father how Opa David shot the wolves and their train trip to Omsk and how cold it is there. Opa David made up a little rhyme about Omsk that goes like this: "Omsky Tomsky, *kaltes Loch, wär Ich nur in Rosental noch,*" which translates to: "Omsky Tomsky, you freezing hole, I wish I was back in Rosental." (It even rhymes in English.)

Now, being back in Rosental, means going to school again. Salomon is not a great scholar. He loves music and fiddling with machinery on Opa David's farm. He also loves horses and secretly hopes that Opa David will give him one, but that never eventuates. Still, he spends much time with his grandfather talking and looking after the horses. School seems to be the place to go when there is nothing else to do. Certainly in the summer and during harvest time, every man, woman, and child is involved in some kind of work, so schooling takes a backseat. The local Russian authorities seem to turn a blind eye to this situation.

Five-year-old Salomon is blissfully unaware of the troubles brewing within Russia. The Bolsheviks are at work on their revolutionary activities, which the Tsar is trying desperately to squash. To do that, he continues to focus on the Jews as being the troublemakers, and the pogroms' frequency and savagery introduce an ugly period in Russian history. For that matter, the Bolsheviks do not have any love for the Jews either and are happy to share in eradicating them. This is putting a great deal of emotional strain on all in the villages, especially those that know they have a Jew in their midst. The villages that the pogroms target are getting ever closer to Rosenthal.

✦

On a pitch-dark, frosty night in mid-February, while everyone is in bed, there is a gentle tapping noise on Friedrich's door. He wakes and listens again, and the tapping continues. Friedrich gets out of bed and, without putting a light on, tiptoes to the front door to listen. There is that tapping again! Friedrich opens the door gently, as a blast of cold air greets him. In the pitch dark he gropes for the doorframe with his hands to guide him out farther.

Suddenly, Friedrich's heart seems to stop when a frozen hand grabs his. He cannot even let out a scream. His voice is gone. The next second, a Russian soldier jumps up and puts his hand over Friedrich's mouth, pushes him back into the house, and shuts the door gently but quickly. Friedrich sits there in total shock. His brain does not even seem to rationalize this event. Then—"Juri! What on earth are you doing? You are scaring the life out of me!" Friedrich suddenly finds a voice.

The Russian soldier kneels in front of Friedrich and says with a soft voice, "Friedrich, you are a good friend. I came here tonight risking my life. If the authorities get to know that I came to warn you, I will be shot for it. So please listen carefully to what I say. Next week there will be a gang of Tsarist supporters who will comb the villages around here to look for Jews. They have done their homework and have set up a spy network to find out who are Jews in these villages. Not everyone in this village is your friend, Friedrich. I have the list, and you are on it. They will probably kill you and your family. Your father, David, is also on the list."

By now Friedrich is starting to comprehend the situation. His mind is racing as panic grips him. Somehow the story of his ancestor Itzhak in Ludwigsburg jumps into his mind. "What should I do, Juri?"

"Very quietly, pack up all your essential goods."

"But what about all that we own here, our business and fields and—"

"And nothing, Friedrich! None of this will be any use to you when you are dead. They are going to take everything anyway. Try to save your life and that of your family. Tomorrow, go and get your father, David, but not in daylight. Do nothing in broad daylight that might rouse suspicion. Take food for two weeks, wrap yourselves in warm clothes, and the day after tomorrow leave here at four in the morning for Saratov. That will be my watch shift. No one is allowed to leave here without my permission. I will simply wave you on when you come past the watch house. Now, speak not a word to anyone except Pauline. Good luck, and may God be with you, Friedrich." The soldier rises, hugs Friedrich, and walks to the door. When he opens it, he looks out furtively to discern whether he can see or hear anyone in the darkness, and then disappears.

As dawn breaks, Friedrich is off to see his father. David is still in bed. When Friedrich explains the dire straits they are in, David says calmly, "Friedrich, I am too old to run away like a fugitive. I have had a good life in Russia—sure, it has had its problems, but I was born here and I want to die here. I am feeling very tired. There are not that many days left in me. Please, leave me here. I will deal with this in my own way and time. Please, Friedrich, be on your way and take care of Pauline and the two children you have. Go and live, Friedrich—live!"

Friedrich hugs his father, and the two men say a tearful goodbye to each other. As Friedrich attempts to leave, David calls out after him, "Friedrich, just before you go, let's have a final drink of vodka together."

When that is done, Friedrich turns resolutely and heads out the front gate of his father's home. A few meters down the road, he hears a single gunshot.

When he arrives home, Pauline is up making breakfast. When Friedrich enters, Pauline is aghast at his appearance. "What has happened to you?"

Friedrich breaks down, grief-stricken and panicky. Pauline quickly sends the children back to bed. When Friedrich recovers sufficiently, he explains all to Pauline. She will have to do most of the packing, while Friedrich will get the coach and horses ready. The coach he has built most recently is for a well-to-do businessman in Krasny Kut. He should deliver it in the next few days but decides to use it for his escape. "Tonight I will go over and bury my father. I cannot leave him. Try and keep the children happy. Tell them one of your stories, while I get the coach ready."

Later that night Friedrich enters David's homestead, where he sees his father's body slumped against the bed. He vomits at the sight. There is a gunshot wound to his head and a pistol near his hand. Friedrich can barely deal with the thought of touching his father. He rakes up all the courage to bury him and at least give him the dignity he deserves. He finds a frost-sheltered area underneath the haystack in the shed where the soil is not completely frozen. He is able to dig a shallow grave and gently places David's body in it and then covers it over. It is almost too much for him to bear. After that he retrieves his father's pistol and some ammunition, runs into the house, and searches for his father's papers. When he locates them, he also finds a wad of rubles, which he takes as well, and makes his way home in the semidarkness. He hopes no one notices him.

Pauline works hard to get everything ready for their escape, despite being five months pregnant. Both pack the wagon and check that all is there. They let the children sleep while they work in the dark to do what they can. They have made a comfortable bed for the children in the back of the carriage. Their belongings are safely packed in the box at the rear. Food and clothing and other personal effects are on the floor. Friedrich checks his watch. It says 3:45 a.m. It's time to get the still-sleepy children and make them comfortable in the back. Pauline and Friedrich are rugged up to face the cold night. They check the time again. It is 3:55 a.m. It is exactly five minutes to the watch house.

A few meters before they reach the watch house, Leopold Jentzen, a village neighbor, steps out of the dark in front of the horses to bring them to a halt. "And where do you think you are going this time of night, my Jewish friend? Don't you know there is a curfew?"

"Where I am going is none of your business, and yes, I do know there is a curfew for some of you, so what are *you* doing out on the street in the middle of the night? Do you suffer from insomnia?"

Juri, who is watching this incident, comes walking over and asks if there is a problem. Jentzen insists that the Hahns have no business being out here. Juri pretends to check Friedrich's papers but secretly slips him some other papers. "Your papers are all in order, Mr. Hahn; you may proceed." He orders Jentzen to go home. When Jentzen is out of sight and earshot, Juri says to Friedrich, "This is a predicament I have not anticipated. You go, Friedrich; I will deal with Jentzen so that he will not be able to reveal this to anyone. My life is at stake also. So I must do what I must do before dawn. *Do svidaniya*, my friend, *do svidaniya!*"

"*Do svidaniya*, Juri. I will never forget your kindness."

By late evening the same day, they reach Engels, where they stay overnight. The next morning, they do the treacherous crossing of the Volga River and arrive in Saratov. Friedrich finds one of his distant cousins, who is still involved in the newspaper business. They stay the night while Friedrich gives him the coach and horses in gratitude for his kindness and for arranging their train trip to Moscow. When the cousin shows him in the newspaper that Prussia is opening its doors to migrants from Russia, their destination is now firmly set and Friedrich plans his trip. The train journey to Moscow in these wintry conditions should take them about four days if the weather is holding. If there are very heavy snowfalls, it may take twice that long.

The train carriages are not exactly first class. The benches are primitive and hard, and heating is spasmodic. On the train are many Germans leaving Russia. In the crowd of so many Germans, Friedrich feels safe as the only Jew among them. However, in Moscow there are delays getting a train to Minsk in Belarus. There are major political unrests and blockades. Russian train tables are at best unreliable but now chaotic. So sleeping at the train station in Moscow is the only way to ensure that if and when a train (any kind of train) should arrive, one has a chance of getting on it.

Eventually, a covered goods train arrives early one morning with several empty carriages. All scramble aboard. There are no real seats—just hard floor space with a little straw to keep out the cold. That trip takes another ten days. The final leg is to Königsberg, the capital city of Prussia. They reach this point on April 22, 1912. In Königsberg, their papers are processed and their money is checked and exchanged for German currency, and when they have established that they have the required amount of money for their entry into Prussia, they are given permission to settle in Masuria. Friedrich is issued an interim work permit and is encouraged to work toward German citizenship as soon as possible.

Chapter 13

From the Frying Pan into the Fire

"Whoever claims to be a wolf must also howl like one."
—*East Prussian Proverb*

FRIEDRICH FINDS SOME CASUAL WORK AS A CARPENTER IN A PLACE CALLED POPIELNEN, a beautiful location on the largest of the Masurian lakes, called the Spirding See. When Elisabeth sees the place, she runs to Pauline and gives her a hug and kisses. "You are so right, Mama. This is just like the place you told me about where I will meet Oma and Opa Meier." Elisabeth runs to the beach of the Spirding See" and looks over the waters, where fishing boats are busy with their catches and a few sailing boats are crisscrossing. Elisabeth is blissfully content to sit there and wait.

"Why are Oma and Opa Meier not coming?" she asks Pauline after some days.

"Well, Elisabeth, there are a thousand lakes here and they may be looking at another lake. We will go to other lakes soon and see if they are there." Elisabeth, now thirteen years old, is realizing that Pauline's story is just a placebo for her to live on until she is old enough to completely understand the tragedy involving her beloved grandparents. Pauline looks into the eyes of Elisabeth, which say, *I know Oma and Opa are dead.* Pauline hugs her and says, "You poor child, I wish we could have protected them from those Russian predators."

On April 30 of that year 1912, Pauline gives birth to her second son, Richard. Wisely, they choose a good Aryan name for him. The following year, in August, their third son is born. Friedrich feels less impelled to give him an Aryan name, as the Jewish problem does not seem to exist here. So he is named Samuel, followed by the next son, born in 1914, named Paul. During the war years of 1914-1918, Friedrich works tirelessly to support the war effort with his specialised coach-building skills, essential for the prosecution of the war. For this he is rewarded with German citizenship, which they receive on April 23, 1917, in the city of Allenstein.

For a while after the war, life takes on a semblance of normality. Friedrich's work becomes well known, and he receives some good contracts to build coaches and do other carpentry work. Elisabeth is now twenty-one years old and is being courted by a so-called "gentleman" named Franz Salewski from Prostken, a Masurian town on the Polish border, thirteen kilometres away from Lyck. Salewski, although always a bit shy of work, manages to persuade Elisabeth to marry him. He has an outgoing personality and loves having fun. However, it is not a great marriage because Franz is also very fond of drinking and women. The result is that Friedrich needs to support his daughter with a bit of extra money whenever he can. There is never much money left for food, and Elisabeth's health begins to suffer.

In the wake of World War I, the political situation in Prussia takes an ugly turn. Because Prussia is now geographically cut off from Germany, the whole region forms an isolationist mentality, much like an island in an ocean. In this situation, the National Socialist Party is able to get hold of this region as it does no other in Germany. Prussia is now the "hotbed" of the party. As the party's extremist views become known, the general population embraces its ideology. Friedrich sees the writing on the wall. He ensures that all his children legally change their names to "Christian" names: Salomon becomes Friedrich, or Fritz, and Samuel becomes Max; the rest already have Aryan names. Still, this action is noted, and it spreads among the party faithful. At first, some people make rude remarks. Gradually, these actions become more overt and people are persuaded not to do business with Friedrich if they are to retain the favor of the party.

As early as 1921, the Lyck newspaper reports on the activities of an anti-Semitic group that later becomes a part of Hitler's National Socialists. It holds a gathering of its members in the city of Lyck, an event the city council sanctions. Among its vicious propaganda is a campaign to drop anti-Semitic leaflets from planes, with a swastika on one side and the slogan "Hit the Jews" on the reverse. Any citizen speaking out against the National Socialists' attitude toward Jews will be identified as a "friend of Jews" and will receive appropriate attention.

During the national election of 1924, this group receives the second-highest number of votes in the district of Lyck. It comes as no surprise, then, that in the spring of 1925 a group of National Socialist henchmen enter Friedrich's workshop. They force him to sell up his shop at ridiculous market prices. Many Jews are now forced out once more, to the larger German cities, where they can have some anonymity to carry on their business. Friedrich quickly chooses to move to a village within Masuria where he may be out of the focus of the National Socialists, to have a chance to make a living for himself and his family. They relocate to a semidetached house in Stradaunen, about five kilometres from the Masurian capital, Lyck. This is a much happier place for them, their fourth son, Horst, is born here, and their daughter, Olga. Friedrich works as a freelance carpenter on various farms. The children have to work on these farms as well, and little time is left for schooling.

While Friedrich suffers physically and emotionally, the children make the best of their new situation. Sure, the work is hard for them, too, but they do have Max, and Max will see the funny side of anything; he mimics the farmer and secretly mocks him. The other boys are, of course, no angels and play up Max's antics. At one point the boys, compose a mocking song about the farmer they work for. In the privacy of their home, they sing it and roll on the floor laughing as they add more lyrics.

Their younger sister, Olga, hears it, of course, and she sings it openly. One of the quirky farm hands, an older Polish man named Vladek, hears Olga singing this song. Since he does not like the boys he becomes upset. So when he sees the farmer, he blurts out angrily, in broken German, something like,"Ich kann nicht Lied auf gnä(digen) Herr" (I can't do song about merciful master.)

The farmer looks puzzled. Then he calls Fritz and asks him, "What is Vladek on about?"

Fritz quickly replies, "He is mad, sir. We are all wondering what he means by that. Take no notice of it; he will get over it." The farmer seems satisfied with that, but the boys are not satisfied with their sister. Poor Olga receives a tirade from them that night. Needless to say, the boys give up composing songs, as this incident is far too close for comfort.

Friedrich struggles on to provide for his family. There is no money left to help poor Elisabeth. That thought and the horrible closure of his workshop send Friedrich into a deep depression. He does not recover from this blow. Until now, he knew how to live with the Russian type of "wolves." But this lot is far more dangerous and cunning. Friedrich knows he is outwitted and defeated. He knows there is nowhere to run or to hide. "*God!*" he cries out loud on his deathbed, while throwing his hands up to heaven in utter despair, he says: "I did not ask to be born a Jew!" These are his last words. He dies an angry and troubled man in 1927, a few months after Elisabeth dies due to her lack of nutrition. They are both buried in the nearby village of Grabnik. The family puts some nice grave markers on their resting places, but the National Socialist Party destroys them, desecrates their burial places, and warns the family not to attempt to replace the grave markers or decorate the graves with flowers and ornaments.

Salomon, as the eldest son, now takes on the role of the provider. He is strong and healthy and earns the respect of the landowner, who rewards him with little extras for his mother and siblings. But Fritz (as he is now known) is also ambitious. He does not want to spend the rest of his life working on farms. He has a good brain and is full of ingenious plans. On one of his trips into Lyck, he sees a second-hand cornet in a pawnshop. He saves enough to buy it and teaches himself to play it by ear. Still, that is not enough. He wants to be a real musician who can read music. So, each time he goes out to plow the fields, he writes, with chalk, music notations on the back of the plow and then memorizes the notations. In a very short while, he has it together and buys some sheet music with popular dance tunes. Then he sets out to teach his brother Max to play the tenor horn and Paul to play the euphonium. After work, they go into the hayshed and practice and practice. Only Richard does not seem to share this love of music.

Fritz's break comes when the Prostken Band is short a cornet player for a concert. Franz Salewski, the drummer of the band, recommends Fritz, and they send for him to have a practice session with them. Max and Paul also come along. Fritz is an instant hit. He brings enormous energy to the band with his powerful playing. Fritz and his brothers quickly gain a reputation as good musicians and fun to work with, mainly because of Max, who is an incurable comedian and a real charmer. All the women love him. This popularity is a great camouflage for their Jewish background. No one ever questions it, not even the Party bosses and the awestruck admirers who come to the dances where the Hahn boys play.

Among those admirers are the Janutta boys, Hermann, Willi, and Rudolph. They are proud Prussians and besotted with their Aryan heritage, claiming to have some of the "bluest Prussian blood" in their veins, supposedly because they are descendants of Wilhelmina, "The Wild One," Duchess of Prussia, albeit through illegitimacy. Hence, they are well cared for in a material way. Now thoroughly indoctrinated with the new socialist dogmas, the boys in the Janutta family embrace anti-Semitism with great vigor, not least to cover their own vulnerability as "blue bloods." Since the expression "blue bloods" refers to being of royal descent, and royalty is an enemy of revolutionary ideologies, they prefer to be known as good "Aryans."

Their only sister, gorgeous Elfriede, often accompanies her brothers to the dances. More to the point, *they* accompany *her* to keep a watchful eye on her, because she is a vivacious, energetic young woman who is extremely popular with young men.

Elfriede is the second-eldest child of Fredericke and Gustav Janutta. She has an older brother called August, from a previous liaison of Fredericke. Elfriede was only eleven years old when her beloved father was killed in February 1917 at Kowel, Russia. She waited at the gate for him for a whole year, hoping he would return to her. She suffered badly. Good-hearted August then took on the role of her mentor and protector. With his care, she has found a measure of comfort and stability.

✧

Along the Lyck See stretches a beautiful promenade, behind which, higher up, are some elegant houses and restaurants. One such popular restaurant is the Stamms Terrasses, with views over the promenade and the lake. The owner of the establishment hires Fritz's band to play every Saturday afternoon and evening. Rudolph Janutta, a brilliant clarinettist, joins the Hahns' band, as does Franz Salewski, the drummer. Franz, however, is the X factor of the band. Whenever he is sober enough, which is not often, he plays the drums well, but his reliability leaves a little to be desired, much to the frustration of Fritz and the other musicians.

On this particular Saturday afternoon, the band sets up and is ready to play. The house is packed, and all are in high spirits, ready to dance the day and night away.

"Where the hell is Franz?" asks Fritz. He is nowhere to be seen. Fritz, who is not known for his patience, wants to go and find Franz and "choke" him.

Then Rudolph taps him on the shoulder and says, "My sister is here; she is happy to drum for us. Shall I call her over?"

Fritz is at once reluctant to play with an unknown drummer and very excited to have Elfriede join him. He has been watching her on the dance floor for the past few weeks, and he fancies her really badly. "All right, Rudi, go and get her."

When she sits down and adjusts the drum kit for herself, with a few flourishes with the drumsticks, the audience begins to giggle. "This is going to be interesting, a girl playing drums in a band—have you ever seen anything like this?" someone says. Fritz checks with her to see if she knows their repertoire. Elfriede just nods her head, flicks her long, wavy hair back, and is rearing to go like a filly ready for a race. When the band rips into the first polka, the audience erupts with applause for Elfriede. They leap to their feet and race to the dance floor. The day is saved. Franz gets the sack from the band. Elfriede has a permanent job with the boys.

Over the next few weeks, the Janutta boys become a little worried when their sister spends a lot of time talking with Fritz in between breaks. They watch as they note a romance blossoming between the two. They find themselves in a predicament. "What if...? To be in the band with the son of a known Jew is one thing, but to have him as our brother-in law? That is unthinkable for us Aryans!" Hermann is raising his concerns. Gradually, they pressure their sister to stop her flirting with a Jew and threaten her with banishment from the band, or worse. Fritz and Elfriede decide to keep a low profile and deal with each other in a nonchalant, casual manner when in public. However, secretly they do meet. Their attraction to each other is very strong, and the inevitable happens: she becomes pregnant. Whom can she turn to now?

Fritz is an honorable man. He wants to marry her. He agrees to meet Elfriede secretly, riding his motorbike to a prearranged place to discuss marriage plans with her. As he is about to drive over to meet his sweetheart, Paul, a young man who lives across the farm from Elfriede, and whom her brothers call a "social misfit," arrives just as Fritz starts to drive off on his motorbike. "Stop, Fritz stooop," Paul yells at the top of his voice. He is on an urgent errand from Elfriede. The message is that under no circumstance should Fritz come to see her tonight, as arranged, but should meet her tomorrow at the post office in Lyck at 3:30 p.m. He passes on the message, which puzzles Fritz, but he accepts it.

They meet the next day. Elfriede is upset and tearful. She relates how she discovered a plot to ambush and kill Fritz. Her brothers met in the barn but were unaware that their sister was up in the loft, where she often spends time reading a book. From there, she watched as each of her brothers took a large, sharp kitchen knife and hid it inside their boots, covered by their trousers. They spoke of an ambush that was to take place that very night on the lonely track that Fritz often uses to visit Elfriede on his motorbike. They want to "kill this Jew who dared to make our sister pregnant," she heard them say. Once they left, she rushed over to Paul and asked him to ride his bike over to warn Fritz.

"We are in extreme danger," says Fritz. "Your brothers will be in a rage over their failed assassination attempt." He now proposes a plan as to how they will have to live among this ferocious bunch of men.

First, they must contact Elfriede's brother August and take him into their confidence. With his help, they arrange to get married on July 12, 1929, in a village near Lyck. Second, they will publicly associate with the boys as if nothing has happened. That includes keeping Rudolph in the band and having a few drinks with him and his brothers. "Love your neighbors—it annoys the hell out of them" is Fritz's rule of thumb. Third, Max and Paul will keep an eye on the Janutta boys to see if they plot another assassination. Fourth, they will keep a high public profile as a deterrent for the

From the Frying Pan into the Fire

Januttas to plot anything. Fritz's instincts on this matter are not wrong.

A few days later, Markus, a young police constable, overhears this threat: "She and her Jew will pay for that—when we are ready," Hermann swears to a Nazi friend at the pub while in a drunken stupor. Markus warns Elfriede. They were good friends as children. Elfriede has grown stunningly beautiful, and Markus still has great love and respect for this woman. He could not bear to see her come to grief.

This new threat calls for quick and decisive action. Four weeks later, she and Fritz are quietly married. They are not intimidated enough by that threat to crawl into a hole, away from the world. No! This is their life, and they want to live it together to the fullest. They are also a very popular couple around town, and that adds a little dimension to their otherwise fragile security. Consequently, the Janutta boys appear to be a bit more accepting of Fritz—at least in public. A kind of unspoken détente ensues.

Now, they try a more covert, if not diplomatic, way to cause a rift between Fritz and Elfriede. Hermann has this brilliant idea. "What if we can trick or embarrass her into joining the National Socialist Party, with its public hatred of Jews?" They bank on the vain hope that Elfriede does not understand the political ideologies of the party and has no idea that they are about to target Jews. They see in this their plan to "get rid of that Jew who disgraced the Janutta name." They are so wrong. To put their plan into action, the Janutta boys actively support preparations for a large rally for the National Socialists in Lyck. The National Socialist elite are invited to address the masses. The Janutta boys suck up to them unashamedly. Elfriede, along with many other women, are ordered to help with the catering. The event is to rouse support for the Party and host a recruitment drive for members.

During the Party boss's euphoric speech, he says, "Is there anyone in this magnificent crowd who does not wish to become a member? Let him go home in shame! You, though, who see a glorious future for Prussia, come and sign up."

A huge crowd of men rush to the front, resembling a crowd at a religious-revival meeting who want to accept Christ as their savior or to receive the Holy Spirit. *But now for the trap*, says Hermann to himself. When that madness subsides, the boss resumes his religious-like, euphoric speech and says, "Women of Prussia - today is the day of all days! You, the mothers of the next generation, who will produce the leaders who make the glory of Prussia shine upon the rest of Germany and all of Europe—the glory that Prussia so rightly deserves—today you can make that dream a reality. Today we want you to be equal members of the Party. When you enrol as a member, you are showing where your heart is—in Prussia and in the ideologies of the Party. Please step forward to join this glorious party."

Women squeal with delight and rush forward to sign up. The Janutta boys watch their sister closely. Will she sign up or embarrass them in front of such dignitaries by not signing? Elfriede holds her breath until she faints. This gets her out of that predicament for the time being. She never joins the women's branch of the National Socialist Party. Fritz is very proud of his wife and praises her loyalty. Having failed in this attempt, the Janutta boys conceive yet another dirty plan. Yes, the "wolf" is a patient hunter.

Chapter 14

Peace and War

"Let him who desires peace prepare for war." —Vegetius

THE SNOW CRUNCHES UNDER HER FEET WITH EACH STEP AS DARKNESS BEGINS TO FALL. It is barely 5:00 p.m. Elfriede is in the third trimester of her pregnancy. The hum of the bus that brought her home from her mother's farm in Mulden fades in the crisp night air. Behind her is the Masurian forest, glistening white in the early moonlight, trees heavily laden with snow and icicles hanging like tiny lanterns from the branches, while the lake, on her left, appears like a table grandly decked with a perfectly white damask tablecloth. By now, Marisha, her Ukrainian maid, will have made the dinner and made Elfriede's home cozy. Thoughts of a warm fire comfort her as the first streetlights of the town of Lyck come into view. Her hand glides over her bulging belly with great delight. "Our child," she says quietly to herself. "But what sort of world will it be born into? What sort of life will it have, when its father is an unwelcome Jew in the eyes of the powers that be?"

This thought seems momentarily as frozen in her brain as the lake is. Then the howling of a pack of wolves in the distance suddenly snaps her out of that terrifying idea. A cold shiver runs down her spine as the eerie sound evokes gruesome images of wolf attacks. Elfriede hates wolves. She has lived among them all the twenty-four years of her life. She hastens her steps as she reaches the street of her home. Suddenly, a booming crack that resembles a cannon shot jolts her. Frozen lakes, such as the one across the road, do that from time to time.

On March 3, 1930, Elfriede gives birth to her first child, a boy, whom they name Heinz. He is a strapping little guy, full of curiosity. He is the pride and joy of his parents. Erika is born some eighteen months later, and followed by another son called Herbert. Erika leaves her brother Heinz for dead, as far as curiosity is concerned. As she is growing up, she earns the dubious title of *Dorfbesen* (the Village Broom), for no one ever knows her whereabouts at any given time. She simply sweeps through the town, talking to anyone who wants to listen to her. Her adventurous spirit knows no bounds.

Erika is about six years old when she takes her baby brother, Herbert, on an outing. By late afternoon, everyone is concerned about where on earth she could be. A search party is organized to find her, but to no avail. Then, as all meet at the brickworks kiln, they hear this plaintive sound in the Polish language: "My God, my God!"

Ears are pitched in every direction, until someone shouts, "There she is—up there!"

All eyes look up to the top of the brickworks stack. There she is indeed, thirty meters above them, clinging with one hand to Herbert on her hip and with the other holding one of the metal rungs that forms steps up to the top. Her parents' hearts leap into their mouths. "Don't move, and don't look down!" they scream.

One of the agile men is already ascending, with another close behind him. When the first one reaches Erika, he grabs Herbert and passes him on to the man below him. Then he gets hold of Erika and they descend with the two children. Back on terra firma, her parents now "get hold" of *her*.

With the arrival of the children, a kind of strange period of peace enters the life of the Hahn family. The home becomes a focal point for the friends' and family's social activities. Many musicians come and go; in time, these include the brothers of Elfriede, who come to play with their nephews and niece. For security reasons, Fritz buys a dog. It is a cross between a German shepherd dog and a wolf. They name him Rolf. He is a great playmate for the children and fiercely loyal to the family, as a few postmen find out. For example, when Elfriede comes down with a potentially fatal disease, which she survives, Rolf never leaves her bedside, other than for the necessary business that dogs must attend to, during all her months of recuperation.

At this time, Hitler makes available to every home a radio receiver at a very low cost. It has only one station—the government station, which broadcasts the speeches of the propaganda minister, Joseph Goebbels, with a little music here and there. It becomes known among the people as Goebbels-Schnauze (Goebbels' Snout), for Goebbels comes on the air anytime without announcements. Thus, one day, while Elfriede is resting with Rolf at her bedside, Goebbels suddenly screams his propaganda across the airwaves. Rolf does not tolerate any intruders, however small they may seem, and jumps onto the radio receiver and smashes it to the ground. Poor Mr. Goebbels!

At Elfriede's behest, Fritz joins the army as a volunteer in the music corps. No one questions his Jewish heritage, as his wise father has already changed his name from Salomon to Fritz after they took on German citizenship. In the army, he meets Karl who is young, tall, blond, and good-looking—very Aryan. Karl has no family. They were all killed in World War I. He grew up in an orphanage and joined the army as soon as he could. While in the orphanage, Karl was sexually abused by one of the supervisors, who bribed him with money and gifts. After leaving the institution, he returned one night and killed the man, Karl confided in Fritz. Fritz, on the other hand, who has never had a close friend, shares with him his innermost thoughts, revealing his Jewish heritage and his fears of the National Socialists. He and Karl become inseparable friends who swear to protect each other come what may.

Karl needs to belong to a family, and he finds it in Fritz's. Besides, they are kindred spirits who share a love of music. Karl is a very fine trombone player, while Fritz plays the tuba, and now both are members of the army music corps. That means being stationed closer to home. This new status not only gives Fritz greater security but also gives Karl more access to a home, a luxury that he begins to enjoy. Warm-hearted Elfriede takes Karl into her family as if he were her own flesh and blood. Karl often stays with Fritz and his family when on leave, and subsequently falls in love with Marisha.

Amid this peace in the family, there are periods of long separation between Fritz and Elfriede. Still they find time for brief reunions. Subsequently, there are born into the family two more sons, Werner in May 1939 and Kurt in December 1940.

❖

For a few years, Germany basks in its military successes. Eventually, its political sabre rattling leads to ominous war clouds that appear on the political horizon. There are disturbing rumors of an imminent invasion of Poland. Lyck, with so many Polish connections, would have its social heart ripped out, if that is to be. Mistrust on both sides of the ethnic-population divide becomes the order of the day and strains personal and business relationships. Amid such unstable conditions, and with Fritz out of the picture, the "pack" sees its real opportunity for revenge.

Early one morning, two vehicles from the SA (*Sturm Abteilung*—a term meaning "Storm Troopers," who were Hitler's secret army, also known as *Brownshirts*) pull up in front of Elfriede's home and "invite" her and the five children to have some "nice photos" taken. However, before going to the town hall for the photos, they take Elfriede to the hairdresser, in one of the adjacent rooms, to cut her lovely long hair so that all her facial features are clearly visible. Ominous! Erika, too, has her hair tied back firmly. The boys always have short hair—no need to cut theirs. They save the SA some money. Although Elfriede knows deep down the reason for the photos, she does ask why they are being taken. An oily SA voice says, "We wish to have a nice photo album of all the families in Lyck for posterity."

As they leave, Elfriede sees a side door slightly ajar. She catches her breath and her heart leaps into her throat when she sees her younger brother Hermann, now a significant officer of the SS (*Schutzstaffel*, Hitler's personal, black-uniformed elite, the volunteer "protection squadron" under the direct command of Heinrich Himmler). *Why is he there?* she wonders. In her heart, she knows the awful truth: this is the "pack's" time for revenge.

Expert geneticists will scrutinize these family photos to see if there are Jewish features in their faces. If there are, that will mean certain deportation to the gas chambers in Auschwitz. Now Elfriede has to wait for the result of their examination. Will the SA arrive one morning and send them to the gas chambers?

Suddenly, a most capricious political wind creates more pressing issues for the SS and the SA than chasing Jews. German troops are massing up along the Prussian-Russian border, ready for a major invasion. Whether because of this political drama or because all the children look much like their mother, nothing follows, much to Elfriede's relief.

❖

The war escalates into full-scale conflict with Poland. Soldiers are sent into various battles, blessed by the chaplains to the tunes Fritz's army band plays. Germany invades Russia, and the German soldiers there commit many atrocities among the populace. Their campaign into Russia brings them to St. Petersburg, and then they retreat. Under the direct orders of the Gauleiter, Erich Koch, the army retrieves the Amber Room from Zarskoje Selo palace and brings it back to Prussia. They set it up in the castle at Königsberg.

In this campaign the German armies not only retrieve the Amber Room but commit unbelievable atrocities on the population, particularly the women. The Russians' rage is implacable. They want vengeance.

Their time comes in the summer of 1944. The Russian soldiers break the border between Russia and Prussia and make an example of the small village of Nemmersdorf. The plundering, rapes, and killings take on the most brutal forms, especially by nailing women by their hands to the barn doors and then raping them until they die. The Russians then withdraw over the border. However, the message to the rest of Prussia is loud and clear. It sends shockwaves through the region, and the women in Lyck begin to flee in panic. Not many men are left now to protect them, because most males have been drafted into the *Volkssturm* (civilian army). Elfriede is well and truly packed and prepares to leave with Marisha and the children. The SA, however, tries to restore calm, promising that the Russians—only eighteen kilometres away—will never reach here. "Unpack, unpack," is the shout of the SA with their drawn pistols.

How Elfriede yearns to have Fritz by her side in this crucial time, but he is a long way from Lyck, having been assigned to the transport division in Berlin. However, Fritz receives news from Elfriede that Karl was left in Lyck with the army to defend the city. It gives him some comfort to know that Elfriede and Marisha have someone to take care of them and the children. The people in Lyck are already feeling the deprivation. Food is being rationed, and other basic items are simply unavailable. Kurt says to his mother, "Mutti, when will we be able to buy everything again?"

"When the war is finished, Kurtchen." (Little Kurt)

"How will we know when the war is finished?"

"Well, there will be people in the streets, shouting and clapping their hands, and the music will play and the big bass drum will beat and everyone will be happy." That seems to satisfy his curiosity for the time being.

Peace and War

Hitler is aware of the Russian armies' massive push toward the Prussian border. Hence, he makes a spectacular entry into Lyck. The people line the streets as he gives his infamous salute, and the crowds respond with a loud "Heil, Hitler." Then the music begins to play and the drum beats and Kurt is beside himself with joy.

"Mutti," he says, "the war is over. I heard the music and the drum. Now we can buy everything again." His mother just hugs him a little tighter.

By the end of summer, it becomes painfully clear that the borders will be broken on two or perhaps three fronts. July 25, 1944, is a day that will be remembered, burned into scarred hearts, forever. "Every woman and child, take one piece of luggage per person and present at the railway station at two p.m. sharp," an official of the NSDAP (National Socialist German Workers' Party) bellows through their loudspeakers at eight o'clock in the morning.

Karl knocks on the front door a few minutes later. "Can I do anything for you?" he asks Elfriede.

"You can come and take us to the railway station around one p.m.," she replies, "and would you please drive to Stradaunen to pick up Oma Pauline and Fritz's sister, Olga?"

"Of course. I should have thought of that myself—so where is Horst?"

"He is in the Hitler Youth camp, training as a paratrooper."

"All right—I'll be on my way." And off he rushes, after giving a very tearful Marisha a hug and a kiss.

"Don't leave me here for the Russians, Karl—promise to take me with you," shouts Marisha, as Karl jumps into the army truck and drives off.

There is chaos at the railway station. People are crying and hugging, asking one another about relatives and friends whom they cannot find here. Bewildered expressions on the faces of children accentuate the confusion. "Only German citizens will be allowed on the train!" comes the announcement.

Karl is assigned to escort the train of sixty carriages, leaving his beloved Marisha behind. "I'll come back to get you, Marisha," he shouts over the general din.

Elfriede's good-bye with Marisha is extremely painful and heart-wrenching for both women, who have come to love and respect each other. Elfriede knows in her heart the ordeal that awaits Marisha once the Russian troops come into the city. "Mrs. Hahn, please don't leave me; please, please, take me with you" are her last words before a German soldier, known to Karl, brutally pushes her away from the train and kicks her with his jackboots. He then leaves her in agony in her crumbling, bleak world. At 3:00 p.m., the trainload is heading north, in the direction of Danzig, for evacuation by ship, via the Baltic Sea, to the German harbor of Kiel, near the Danish border.

✦

After barely four hours, the train journey is abandoned, still a long way away from Danzig. Elfriede and her children are sent to work on a farm for an indefinite period. Summer passes, as does autumn, and the cold winter sets in. The Russian troops make further progress into Prussia. Karl is sent temporarily to Danzig to assist with the evacuation onboard the ship *Wilhelm Gustloff* and other Vessels. Several successful trips by the *Wilhelm Gustloff* bring thousands of refugees to Germany. However, January 30 proves to be her last voyage, to an icy, watery grave with all ten thousand onboard. Just hours after leaving Gotenhafen, and in pitch darkness, three Russian submarine torpedoes rip into the side of the ship, hitting it where the nurses are looking after wounded soldiers. They have no chance.

Lifeboats are loaded with women and children and top-ranking Nazis. The launching of these lifeboats is an unmitigated disaster. A number of mechanical problems arise because the ropes lowering the lifeboats partway down the ship are frozen. In an attempt to force the issue, most of the lifeboats simply capsize, emptying the horrified people into the frozen waters and to their certain death. Lifeboats that actually make it safely into the water are surrounded by people, both dead and those clinging desperately to the boats. The shock is simply too much for some, and in a fit of madness they even jump out of the lifeboat to their death. Some of the SS and SA personnel simply take the easy way out. Here and there is heard a pistol shot, followed by a splash in the water. As the ship lists more and more, there is no choice left—jump or go down with the ship.

One of the last to jump into the icy water is a nurse who struggles against the water rushing down on her. When she reaches the top deck, the ship is about to sink. She jumps fully clothed into the water and swims some fifty meters, when the ship suddenly goes below, creating a "drag" as it sinks. The nurse struggles with all her might not to go down with it. In a few minutes, she is picked up by a minesweeper that comes to rescue the hapless victims of the stricken vessel. She survives to tell the story while the cries for help gradually perish into an eerie silence. Among the victims are relatives of the Hahn family. The dawn reveals the full horror: bodies covering the surface of the sea. Other lifeboats that did manage to get launched but are not discovered until first light in the morning float aimlessly, full of frozen bodies. Very few people survive. It is the greatest disaster in maritime history.

✦

For the masses that are left on the farms, it is now too late to make it to Danzig. "There are no more trains to Danzig, and all roads are blocked. Only those who have made it there will eventually be evacuated by ship," announces Karl upon his return, unaware of the tragedy that will shortly unfold on the Baltic Sea. He speaks of going back to Lyck to find Marisha, but hesitates to go. First, he has another promise to keep. Westward is their only escape route now, and it proves to be a horrific and bewildering journey. By whatever means of transport that is available, or on foot, heaving masses of people are on the move—a pitiful sight. Karl keeps an eye on Elfriede and the children; sometimes he even carries the youngest ones, who are hungry and exhausted. Food becomes a luxury, and many elderly ones and babies die on this journey. Still, the worst is yet to come.

Around 2:00 p.m. on December 20, 1944, a train is ready to leave for an undisclosed destination somewhere in Pomerania. The train is traveling overnight and stops at a place called Flatow, near the fuel depot with its large tanks of petrol. Werner and Kurt are awake, as are most passengers on that train. Suddenly the night calm is ripped apart by an enormous explosion as one fuel tank after another explodes, changing night into day in the ensuing inferno. The heat is unbearable, as the paint on the train is blistering. Quickly the train pulls away to a safer place. Later they learn that some German soldiers sabotaged the fuel storage tanks to prevent the advancing Russian army from taking advantage of it.

In the morning, all passengers are transferred to a number of waiting trucks and taken to the nearby village of Kappe, which has been all but abandoned by its residents. In the ensuing chaos, Elfriede is separated from her mother-in-law, Pauline, and her daughter, Olga. There is no trace of them, and she hopes and prays that they are safe, somewhere. Elfriede and the children are given an empty, cold, and dilapidated house to stay in. The NSDAP party people have taken the best places for themselves. Now Elfriede's rage is at its best. She confronts the party boss, and within one hour she has beds and some furniture in the house. She scrubs and whitewashes the entire place to make it liveable and respectable. Outside, the snow is falling heavily. The children are delighted to go tobogganing down any slope they can find on whatever piece of wood that might suit. The other delight for them is no school! An SS tank division has taken over the village school.

Peace and War

Fritz's annual leave is due around Christmastime. By December 26, he finally meets up with his family here in Kappe. The reunion is joyful. The only sad bits are that Pauline and Olga are missing, and that Heinz is not here with them, as he is still in Berlin at the school of music. Since Karl made it here also, he sees his friend Fritz again. The men are happy to see each other again and have a little celebration. Elfriede tells Fritz just how helpful Karl has been. "I love your family so much, Fritz; I would do anything to keep them safe and sound," says Karl. "I was hoping to deliver them into your arms. Now that you are here, my mission is finished. I'm going back to Lyck. I can't get the picture of Marisha being thrown onto the railway station platform out of my mind. I am going back in the hope of finding her or that horrible soldier who was so cruel to her. I will deal with him in my own way—I think you understand my kind of justice, Fritz. If I make it, well and good; if not, I have nothing to lose. My life has no meaning in this mess. So good-bye, Fritz, and may God take care of you and your family." The men hug each other, and then Karl hugs and kisses the children and Elfriede and leaves.

"What an example of a loyal friend amid a world of disloyalty," says Fritz as he waves good-bye to Karl

In preparation for leaving here again, along with the few remaining people in Kappe, the farmers want to kill their pigs for meat, but there seems to be no one who knows how to butcher a pig. Fritz and Elfriede have such expertise and offer their services in return for some sausages, speck, and fat, to replenish the pot of fat that Elfriede took with her when leaving Lyck. Everything is done in great haste. "God help us if the Russians catch us," says Fritz. That seems to summarize the feelings of the entire village.

On January 3 comes the order to evacuate. The SS tank division has secretly abandoned the village some two days ago to make its escape, leaving the masses of refugees unprotected from the inevitably advancing Russian armies. Once more, panic sets in as everyone is busy packing their gear—mostly food and warm clothes. The Hahn family is loaded onto an open trailer pulled by a tractor. Their destination is some thirty kilometers away, a town called Schneidemühl, where the last train out of Pomerania will leave on January 6 at twelve noon.

The weather and the road conditions on the trip are atrocious. A long colony of "possible" and "impossible" vehicles makes its way slowly toward their goal. High snow and freezing temperatures make the progress very slow. It is not long before the frozen road takes its toll on the tractor in the negative-thirty-degrees-Celsius temperature. The drive shaft breaks with twenty kilometers to go. Fritz decides to keep moving on foot. Any distance between the refugees and the Russians is good. Elfriede lugs the earthenware pot of fat, which weighs around ten kilograms, while the rest of the family carries what is physically possible.

A few kilometers on, a truck comes along, heading toward Schneidemühl, which has a little room for Elfriede and Erika. However, there is a sled that hangs on the side of the truck, so Werner and Kurt are tied onto the sled, wrapped in a blanket, and dragged behind the truck with a rope "glued" to Elfriede's hands. Elfriede and the children are to spend the night on the train that is ready to load the refugees and wounded soldiers. Fritz and Herbert decide not to follow the road for safety reasons but to go cross-country on foot, to make it well in time for the train's departure by twelve noon the next day. Meanwhile, it is 5:00 p.m. and darkness is descending rapidly, when Fritz detects an empty house near an abandoned sawmill. Because of the possibility of wolf attacks, they decide to stay overnight in the safety of the house. And what a find that is! The house has been abandoned just hours earlier and is still warm and well stocked with food. Fritz makes a hearty meal for himself and Herbert before retiring to a warm bed.

Around midnight, a sudden commotion outside makes Fritz jump out the bed, only to find a pack of wolves tearing into a barrel of pickled meat. Fritz thinks how wise the decision to stay indoors proved to be. While Herbert goes back to sleep from sheer exhaustion, Fritz is very uneasy. At 2:00 a.m. he is standing at the window, listening intently for any indication of trouble. Suddenly he calls, "Quickly, son, get up. We have to leave immediately—I can hear the hum of the Russian T-34 tanks in the distance." The crystal-clear night air carries the unmistakable sound of advancing tanks. They have a quick breakfast, and around 4:00 a.m. they leave. Fritz takes the backpack and a case, now full of food, while Herbert carries his father's rifle. The progress is very slow, as Herbert's little legs have difficulty plowing through the knee-high snow. For Herbert, these are the longest five kilometres ever.

At first light, they reach the outskirts of the town. But where is the train station? Eventually they find someone who gives them directions and indicates that it is about a half hour walk from where they are now. What a beautiful sight to see the train! But that thought is quickly shattered when they hear the train whistle blow, indicating its immediate departure—and it is only 9:00 a.m. "Now we have to run," Fritz calls to Herbert. Fritz dumps his backpack with all the goodies and grabs his rifle off Herbert, and together they chase the already slowly moving train. Elfriede hangs out of the carriage window to grab Herbert and pulls him up while Fritz manages to climb aboard after throwing his rifle into the carriage. The train is hopelessly overcrowded, as it is indeed the last one leaving Pomerania. The reason for the early departure is partly that there simply is no more room on the train and the T-34 tanks are menacingly close. Those left behind are at the mercy of the advancing "wolves."

Chapter 15

Rail Tracks of Life and Death

"Escaped the thunder and fell into the lightning." —Spanish Proverb

THE ATMOSPHERE IN THE CARRIAGE IS STIFLING. Twenty wounded soldiers are cramped on one end on some straw. The smell of their injuries fills the carriage and mixes with the stench of the unwashed bodies of another forty civilians—mostly women and children who huddle in the corners. Sanitation is a hit-or-miss effort. When the train stops, it is also a toilet stop for all. When the train does not stop for hours on end, one corner becomes the toilet, which will be cleaned up at the next stop. Water is plentiful, with so much snow around. Windows and doors are closed to keep out the bitterly cold air, while the potbellied stove provides some warmth if there is any firewood. A few potatoes form a small heap on which the most vulnerable sleep, as it provides a little insulation from the freezing floorboards. Other carriages are not so lucky; in these are no stoves at all. Food supplies quickly diminish, and hunger becomes the order of the day. It is not long before the first bodies are unceremoniously thrown out of the moving train into the snowdrifts along the railway tracks.

Fritz and Elfriede's only consolation is that they are with the children in the same carriage. However, some soldiers die of their injuries all alone, without a loved one to hold their hand. They are forgotten when they are thrown out of the carriage. Then a terrible drama unfolds one early morning. Kurt awakens to the screaming of a woman who wants to jump out of the train. He is terrified by her mad behavior and by the force that Fritz uses on her to restrain her from jumping out. Years later, Kurt is told that this woman fell asleep from exhaustion with her baby in her arms. Unfortunately, there was not enough fuel for the stove and the fire went out. The woman was sleeping near a door that had a little gap. The draft froze the baby to death. Fritz, as the only military officer in the carriage, had the unpleasant task of ordering the baby to be thrown out of the carriage. The distraught mother wanted to jump out and die there with her child.

Elfriede tries to pacify Kurt by singing to him. Holding him safely in her arms, she sings an old Masurian song called "Land of Dark Forests and Crystal Lakes." The melody, along with the terror in his little heart, is etched so deeply in his memory that he will never forget it. Just hearing the first few notes of this tune evokes a dark sadness in him. Yet hunger, cold, and sickness are not the only enemies.

In a matter of days, the Russian fighter bombers advance enough to fly overhead in attempts to bomb the train. This alters drastically any plans of escape. From now on the train will travel only at night and without lights, at a very slow tempo. During the day, it stops in a forest or a village that provides some camouflage. The advantage of the daytime stops is that wood for the locomotive and for any stoves can be gathered. Some of the older boys are sent out to find abandoned houses to search for food. The travellers have a veritable feast one day when the train stops in a village. The boys find a bakery that offers to bake a batch of loaves of bread for the train at no cost. They return at the appointed time and collect the "treasure." The disadvantage is that the T-34 tanks make greater progress than the train and are threateningly close behind. It becomes a fine balancing act of passenger survival and risk-taking for the train drivers and those in charge of the evacuation. Can they hold their nerve, allowing the T 34 tanks to gain some distance on them while they stop for food supplies? At times the train will take the risk of driving a certain distance, even during the day, if the tanks are too close for comfort. That presents a real risk to the boys who are ordered off the train to collect wood and food, for the train may move on without notice.

There are days on end when there is absolutely nothing to eat. Elfriede then gives her children a tablespoon full of the fat in her pottery jar. At least they have something in their stomachs, and this gives them some immunity. Amazingly, all in the carriage bear their hunger and privations with great dignity. There are no atheists on this train. Often the prayers of suffering people can be heard in the night. They have no one to turn to except God in their utter despair. Dying soldiers request someone to pray for them, a task that falls mostly on Elfriede.

When the train reaches a village called Kreuz—appropriately named, for it is a crossing of the rail network—Fritz must leave the train to make his way back to his unit in Berlin. A very traumatic and tearful good-bye ensues, with reassurances that he will meet his family again, probably in Hamburg, the given destination at that point in time—that is, if they all survive. The train then proceeds to Stargard, where the Red Cross provides bowls of hot pea soup.

Suddenly, life becomes even more precarious. Ahead of the train are the Allies with their tanks and jet bombers. The train is the figurative meat in the sandwich. Now it is literally squeezed form both sides and it has to go in a north-easterly direction, back toward the Russians but through a gap toward the Baltic Sea. There, in a place called Regenwalde, a refugee camp is set up, and for a couple of days some "normality" returns, in that some food and bedding is available. As expected, in a few days, the news reaches the travellers of the Russians coming toward them. However, when the news of the sinking of the *Wilhelm Gustloff* reaches them it creates an outpouring of grief for the refugees in the camp, for many have friends and relatives that would have been on that ship.

Back on the train—this time in luxury, on a passenger train. Now under aerial attack from both the Russian and the Allied bombers, they find themselves again with daytime stoppages and night-time travel. When the air suddenly begins to vibrate with that familiar hum from the approaching bomber squadrons, the fear on the faces of the refugees on the train resembles that of a person taken to a gallows to be hung. This wave of terror repeats time after time, with demoralizing consequences. Despite all of this, the train makes good progress each night and eventually arrives at a place called Stade, not far from Hamburg, on February 20, 1945. Finally! What a relief! At last among their own people! Or so they think.

❖

When Fritz returns to his unit in Berlin, he is drafted into the transport division. There is no more time for music. It is literally *finita la musica*, as the Italians say. To start with, he has various dangerous transport missions to run. On one such occasion, he is returning to Berlin, when suddenly Allied bombers catch him driving through a village near Berlin. He stops the truck and dives out into a cellar opening between the footpath and a house. His faithful dog, Rolf, makes a split-second decision to get back into the truck. The bomber pilot is an accurate marksman. There is nothing left of the truck, including Rolf. Fritz survives, as he is lying well below street level, but is covered in debris.

When he returns to Berlin, his new assignment is to drive top-ranking Nazi bosses over the Alps to the Italian border. There, they are warmly received by religious clergy in their pompous paraphernalia, who provide them with new identity papers and ship them off to South America. Fritz makes several trips with this kind of "cargo." However, the last trip is particularly traumatic and fateful.

Rail Tracks of Life and Death

In his truck, Fritz has as a co-driver a Russian POW. Since Fritz speaks Russian fluently, they become good friends. Fritz loves the Russian personality, which he has come to know from his childhood days in Rosental. Next to Fritz sits the Nazi boss. As they approach the Italian border, the Nazi boss orders Fritz and his co-driver to stop and get out. He draws his pistol, holds it to the POW's head, and pulls the trigger. Fritz stands there frozen with shock. He expected to be the next one. However, the Nazi boss goes to the truck, picks up a shovel, throws it to Fritz, and says, "Here, burry that swine!" He then stands there with his drawn pistol and watches until Fritz has buried the POW, before ordering Fritz to get into the truck and to continue driving his "toxic cargo" to the border. All the while, he points his pistol at Fritz's head.

"You may as well put it down, sir," Fritz says. "If you pull the trigger, I will have enough presence of mind to turn the wheel sharply left over the sheer drop."

The Nazi boss looks down the cliff and puts his pistol into its holster but never takes his eyes off Fritz. As they reach the border, the Nazi boss jumps out and runs into the arms of the waiting clergy.

The return trip is Fritz's last for the German army. He is captured by American soldiers who have blocked the road. They arrest him and take him to a POW camp in Bavaria, southern Germany. In comparison with the Germans he has had to deal with of late, the Americans are "gentlemen." As it turns out, his stay in the POW camp is short-lived. The American troops are preparing for their Fourth of July celebration, and musicians are in short supply. Fritz is ordered to present himself for rehearsals, a few days before the event, in a place called Hamborn, some eighty kilometers from the camp. To facilitate this, the American army issues him a rail pass that states the destination and the distance.

Well, thank you very much, thinks Fritz, who changes *Hamborn* to *Hamburg* and *80 kilometres* to *800 kilometres*. He presents himself at the railway station and asks for a train to Hamburg, but there is none, only a goods train. He boards that train, sitting outside on the back steps of the carriage, and says, "*Au revoir, mes amis!* It was nice knowing you." A railway track of life, harrowing as the journey is, takes him to Hamburg, where he reports to the Red Cross, which quickly locates his family in a small village near Stade, along the Elbe River.

Walking along the cobblestone road in the village of Ritsch, he notes with great surprise the prosperity of the village and the farms. He knows that Hamburg was badly damaged in the Allies' bombing raids, but this looks more like paradise. The bombers flew over this stretch of very fertile land and spared the farmers most of the war deprivations. The only damage sustained is from the odd ordinance (a military term meaning bombs or explosives) the bombers forgot to drop on Hamburg and then unloaded near the villages on the Elbe River. Thus, the farmers resist with great irritability any inconvenience the German military has placed upon them, such as forcing them to take in POWs on their farms or, worse still, refugees, seen as the scum of the earth. They make no secret of their hatred of these refugees, or *Flüchtlinge*.

Fritz finds his family, which is placed on one of the farms in Ritsch. What a joyful reunion that proves to be. All are there except Heinz, who is still missing. Oma Pauline has been located and is here too, as well as Fredericke, Elfriede's mother.

A *new life at last*, he hopes. Whatever adversity may come, he and his family will be able to deal with it. After all they have been through, surely there cannot be anything new. But he is wrong. Systematic indoctrination into hating the refugees permeates the whole village. No one is certain who or what is behind such a movement. It is not long before the answer arrives.

A few weeks after Fritz's reunion with his family, there is a knock on the door one evening. There stands a very well-fed clergyman from the local community, here to do his "pastoral" duties. The family has just started their dinner, which is very humble fare. The clergyman steps inside and says nothing for what seemed an eternity. Then he walks up to the table and pushes the food to one side with his elbow to make room for his rather large posterior. Folding his arm, he says, "Well, where in the hell did the devil get you swine from?"

Fritz and Elfriede can hardly believe what they have just seen and heard. To call a German a swine is among the greatest insults that can be handed out to him. And Fritz, a powerfully built man with a short fuse, is not to be tampered with. His instinctive dislike for clergy, based on what he saw in the war, boils over like a raging volcano that knows no bounds. He leaps from the table and with his strong hands chokes the clergyman on the floor. Elfriede and Fredericke tried to pull Fritz off him. Fritz loosens his grip, stands up, and tries to get his composure back. The clergyman also stands, unsure on his feet. With that, Fritz's rage comes over him anew. He grabs the clergyman by his pants and his collar and races him to the front door, where he unceremoniously disposes of him in the ditch just outside the front door. That act seems to calm his rage.

He then addresses his family. "We have had all sorts of enemies, and we always knew who they were. We learned to live among them with caution and survived. This type is new to us. We don't understand their thinking. Hence, I do not want religion in my house—ever. Is that clear? What you do outside is your business, but under my roof, we will not speak of anything religious. Otherwise, you will have to depart in the same manner as this insolent clergyman."

The family is stunned. Religion has always been their safe haven in times of trouble, but now it has turned out to be another predator among which they have to live.

Now what will the future hold for them? Life will be different. On the one hand, in the aftermath of the war, there are many disillusioned people who have lost family members, friends, and all possessions. Some have lost faith in God and government. On the other hand, it creates new opportunities for predators to exploit the vulnerable and the young. It spawns people who are desperate, greedy, and ruthless. It gives rise to a dog-eat-dog mentality that has lost sight of God and all restraints that a religious conscience may otherwise impose upon people. For the Hahn family, an uncertain future awaits. One thing that they can rely upon is that life will be—as it always has been for them, and is right now—precarious. They will continue "living among wolves."

THE END

Epilogue

As the baby in my family, I grew up in the post-war years of the German reconstruction being branded a "refugee," a title that was unbearable for a sensitive child like me. Adults and my peers alike used this term as an insult. We were second-class citizens among our own people. There were continually conflicts between the locals and the "refugees" for many years. This made learning in school very difficult, since survival on the playground and after school, on the way home, was paramount and occupied my mind. Subsequently, I was forced to leave school after year eight.

For a while I worked in a number of trades, but my heart was not in them. All along, I was developing a burning desire to become a musician. I also loved writing stories. Eventually my father enrolled me in a very old, traditional school of music in Hamburg-Harburg with Mr. Brigatt, the director, who was like a drill sergeant to the students. This highly structured regime suited me very well. Here, I qualified as an orchestral musician.

My father, who worked for the German railways, was also desperate to get back to playing music, but circumstances were not favorable for him. He was a good provider for the family and the two grandmothers who lived with us permanently. My father and I became very close friends because of our common love of music. Eventually we were able to play in the same orchestra on a part-time basis. It was during this time that my father revealed a little about himself, though he was always cautious not to overstep the agreement made years ago in Masuria between the adults of the family, to keep the children from the truth about our Jewish heritage. However, it was eventually revealed to us on my mother's deathbed. Then I was able to put together the pieces that were like an incomplete jigsaw puzzle.

For example, one day, on the way to a rehearsal, my father said to me, "Son, I want you to get out of Germany. Please don't stay here. Go and make a life for yourself. Don't even marry a German, so that you have no ties to this country." At the time, this had a very romantic overtone and I did not hear the danger in his voice. However, he had planted the seed in my mind, and it grew.

On Monday, January 12, 1959, I was involved in a head-on collision of two metropolitan buses in Hamburg-Wilhelmsburg. The smaller of the two buses, in which I was, ran into a snowdrift and subsequently spun around in the direction of the larger bus coming the other way. I was hospitalized for a while and then sent home to recuperate from my knee injury. It was on one of these boring days that I read in the local paper an ad with the headline "Australia Wants You." Immediately I heard the voice of my father in my head: *Get out of Germany.* I applied for the immigration papers and furiously worked on my next-eldest brother, Werner, to persuade him to join me in this venture. Eventually I won out, and he applied also. He was accepted, but I was not. He was a qualified boilermaker and I a musician. The simple equation was: they did not need musicians; they needed tradesmen. However, when I produced a certificate that I was a qualified boilermaker-welder, all went according to plan.

Werner and I arrived in Australia on July 21, 1959, onboard a very small ship called the *Aurelia*. Two years later, Werner married Sydney lass, Rhonda Grigg. He continued working as a boilermaker until his retirement, raising a family of three boys. As for me, I married a farmer's daughter from Goulburn named Melva Peters, and we raised two daughters, Tania and Anita. To support my family, I worked in a number of industries but always did some performance work with Australian theatres, the Australian Ballet Orchestra, and the Sydney Elizabethan Theatre Trust Opera Company orchestra, and other musical freelance work. Later, I lectured part-time in music at the University of Western Sydney, where I qualified as a schoolteacher. For some twenty years I taught Music in Canberra's High Schools. Here I also started the School Jazz Band movement in this city. For twenty-four years, I also occupied myself as a freelance journalist and a composer of varying styles of music.

Retired now, I am a grandfather to nine and a great-grandfather to sweet little Lily, and, having experienced the roll-on effects of my ancestry, I am grateful that I have been able to break the vicious two-hundred-year-old cycle of my family's having to "live among wolves" and forever run away from them. I now live in Canberra, Australia, with my wife, Mellie, where life without "wolves" has been very kind to me and my descendants. I thank my father for his deep insight.

Epilogue

1. Schaffhausen	11. Susannental	19. Fischer
2. Clarus	12. Kind	20. Philippsfeld
3. Bettinger	13. Näb	21. Paulskoje
4. Basel	14. Brockhausen	22. Enders
5. Zürich	15. Hockerberg	23. Nieder-Monjou
6. Wittmann	16. Orlowskoje	
7. Schönchen	17. Obermonjou	
8. Zug	18. Beauregard	
9. Luzern		
10. Unterwalden		

The German villages of the Wolgagebiet

Printed in Great Britain
by Amazon